U.S. Fish & Wildlife Service

2011 National Survey
of Fishing, Hunting,
and Wildlife-Associated Recreation

Indiana

FHW/11-IN
Issued March 2013

2011 National Survey of
Fishing, Hunting, and
Wildlife-Associated Recreation

Indiana

U.S. Department of the Interior
Ken Salazar,
Secretary

U.S. Fish and Wildlife Service
Dan Ashe,
Director

U.S. Department of Commerce
Rebecca M. Blank,
Acting Secretary

Economics and Statistics Administration
Vacant,
Under Secretary for Economic Affairs

U.S. CENSUS BUREAU
Thomas L. Mesenbourg,
Acting Director

ECONOMICS
AND STATISTICS
ADMINISTRATION

**Economics and Statistics
Administration
Vacant,**
Under Secretary for
Economic Affairs

**U.S. CENSUS BUREAU
Thomas L. Mesenbourg,**
Acting Director

**U.S. Department of the Interior
Ken Salazar,**
Secretary

**U.S. Fish and Wildlife Service
Dan Ashe,**
Director

**Wildlife and Sport Fish Restoration
Hannibal Bolton,**
Assistant Director

The U.S. Department of the Interior protects and manages the Nation's natural resources and cultural heritage; provides scientific and other information about those resources; and honors its trust responsibilities or special commitments to American Indians, Alaska Natives, and affiliated Island Communities. The mission of the Department's U.S. Fish and Wildlife Service is working with others to conserve, protect, and enhance fish, wildlife, and their habitats for the continuing benefit of the American people. The Service is responsible for national programs of vital importance to our natural resources, including administration of the Wildlife and Sport Fish Restoration Programs. These two programs provide financial assistance to the States for projects to enhance and protect fish and wildlife resources and to assure their availability to the public for recreational purposes. Multistate grants from these programs fund the National Survey of Fishing, Hunting, and Wildlife-Associated Recreation.

Suggested Citation

U.S. Department of the Interior, U.S. Fish and Wildlife Service, and U.S. Department of Commerce, U.S. Census Bureau. 2011 National Survey of Fishing, Hunting, and Wildlife-Associated Recreation.

Contents

List of Tables

Foreword

When I was growing up, it was taken as a matter of faith that kids belonged outside. I grew up with 4 brothers, and during those long, hot Atlanta summers, it was common for our mom to holler, "You boys get outside, and don't come back 'til it's dark." It never occurred to me or my brothers to do anything else in our spare time but explore the world around us. The truth is, we had little else to do. But those experiences – waking up on frosty mornings and starting the campfire, scanning trees for a shot at a scampering gray squirrel in the dawn light, scouring creek beds for crawdads and other fishing bait, or simply of the fun we had tramping through the forest – shaped who I am, and drew me to a career in conservation.

That's why I'm excited by this 2011 National Survey of Fishing, Hunting, and Wildlife-Associated Recreation. This report, the 12th in a series that began in 1955, documents a significant resurgence in the number of people embracing America's Great Outdoors. Hunting participation has increased by 9 percent, while angling participation grew by 11 percent. Nearly 38 percent of Americans participated in wildlife-related recreation, an increase of 2.6 million participants from the 2006 Survey.

In addition, wildlife-related recreation is a major driver of the nation's economy. The 2011 Survey estimates that Americans spent $145 billion on related gear, trips, licenses, land acquisition or leases, and other purchases, representing about one percent of the nation's gross domestic product. This spending creates thousands of jobs, supports countless local communities and provides vital funding for conservation.

This year marks the 75th anniversary of the Wildlife and Sport Fish Restoration Program, a cornerstone of wildlife conservation in the United States. Through excise taxes on firearms, ammunition, archery and angling equipment, the U.S. Fish and Wildlife Service has distributed over $14 billion for State and territorial wildlife conservation programs.

This report would not have been possible without the combined efforts of state wildlife agencies – which provided financial support through the Multi-State Conservation Grant Programs – the Association of Fish and Wildlife Agencies and a number of major national conservation organizations. We also owe our gratitude to the thousands of survey respondents from households across America. Because of you, this Survey is the nation's definitive wildlife-related recreation database and information source concerning participation and purchases associated with hunting, fishing and other forms of wildlife-associated recreation nationwide.

The Fish and Wildlife Service is dedicated to connecting people and families with nature. We are proud to celebrate the good news in this report, and we look forward to continuing progress as we work with the States, and all our partners and the public to help keep recreational fishing, hunting, and wildlife watching growing and going strong.

Dan Ashe
Director, U.S. Fish and Wildlife Service

Survey Background and Method

The National Survey of Fishing, Hunting, and Wildlife-Associated Recreation (Survey) has been conducted since 1955 and is one of the oldest and most comprehensive continuing recreation surveys. The Survey collects information on the number of anglers, hunters, and wildlife watchers, how often they participate, and how much they spend on their activities in the United States.

Preparations for the 2011 Survey began in 2008 when the Association of Fish and Wildlife Agencies (AFWA) asked the Fish and Wildlife Service to coordinate the twelfth National Survey of wildlife-related recreation. Funding came from the Multistate Conservation Grant Programs, authorized by Wildlife and Sport Fish Restoration Acts, as amended.

Four regional technical committees were set up under the auspices of AFWA to ensure that State fish and wildlife agencies had an opportunity to participate in all phases of survey planning and design. The committees were made up of agency representatives.

We consulted with State and Federal agencies and nongovernmental organizations such as the American Sportfishing Association and National Shooting Sports Foundation to determine survey content. Other sportspersons' organizations and conservation groups, industry representatives, and researchers also provided valuable advice.

Data collection for the Survey was carried out in two phases by the U.S. Census Bureau. The first phase was the screen which began in April 2011. During the screening phase, the Census Bureau interviewed a sample of 48,600 households nationwide, to determine who in the household had fished, hunted, or wildlife watched in 2010, and who had engaged or planned to engage in those activities in 2011. In most cases, one adult household member provided information for all members. The screen primarily covered 2010 activities while the next, more in-depth phase covered 2011 activities. For more information on the 2010 data, refer to Appendix B.

The second phase of data collection consisted of three detailed interview waves. The first wave began in April 2011 concurrent with the screen, the second in September 2011, and the last in January 2012. Interviews were conducted with samples of likely anglers, hunters, and wildlife watchers who were identified in the initial screening phase. Interviews were conducted primarily by telephone, with in-person interviews for respondents who could not be reached by phone. Respondents in the second survey phase were limited to those who were at least 16 years old. Each respondent provided information pertaining only to his or her activities and expenditures. Sample sizes were designed to provide statistically reliable results at the state level. Altogether, interviews were completed for 11,330 anglers and hunters and 9,329 wildlife watchers. More detailed information on sampling procedures and response rates is found in Appendix D.

Comparability With Previous Surveys

The 2011 Survey's questions and methodology were similar to those used in the 2006, 2001, 1996, and 1991 Surveys. Therefore, the estimates are comparable.

The methodology for these Surveys differs significantly from the 1955 to 1985 Surveys, so these estimates are not directly comparable to those of earlier surveys. Changes in methodology included reducing the recall period over which respondents had to report their activities and expenditures. Previous Surveys used a 12-month recall period which resulted in greater reporting bias. Research found that the amount of activity and expenditures reported in 12-month recall surveys was overestimated in comparison with that reported using shorter recall periods.

Highlights

Introduction

The National Survey of Fishing, Hunting, and Wildlife-Associated Recreation reports results from interviews with U.S. residents about their fishing, hunting, and wildlife watching. This report focuses on 2011 participation and expenditures of persons 16 years of age and older.

The Survey is a snapshot of one year. The information it collected tells us how many people participated and how much they spent on their activities in the State in 2011. It does not tell us how many anglers, hunters, and wildlife watchers there were because many do not participate every year. For example, based on information collected in the Survey's household screen phase, we can estimate that about 51 percent more anglers and 44 percent more hunters participated nationally in at least 1 of the 5 years prior to the screen survey year 2010.

In addition to 2011 estimates, we also provide trend information in the Highlights section and Appendix C of the report. The 2011 numbers reported can be compared with those in the 1991, 1996, 2001, and 2006 Survey reports because they used similar methodologies. The 2011 estimates should not be directly compared with results from Surveys conducted prior to 1991 because of changes in methodology to improve accuracy.

The report also provides information on participation in wildlife recreation in 2010, particularly of persons 6 to 15 years of age. The 2010 information is provided in Appendix B. Information about the Survey's scope and coverage is in Appendix D. The remainder of this section defines important terms used in the Survey.

This report does not provide information about the State's wildlife resources. That, and additional information on wildlife-related recreation, may be obtained from State fish and wildlife agencies. The Association of Fish and Wildlife Agencies can provide the addresses and telephone numbers of those agencies. The Association's website is www.fishwildlife.org.

Additionally, this report does not provide information about the State's number of licensed anglers and hunters. Historical license data can be found at wsfrprograms.fws.gov.

Wildlife-Related Recreation

Wildlife-related recreation is fishing, hunting, and wildlife-watching activities. These categories are not mutually exclusive because many individuals participated in more than one activity. Wildlife-related recreation is reported in two major categories: (1) fishing and hunting, and (2) wildlife watching, which includes observing, photographing, and feeding fish or wildlife.

Sportspersons

Anglers   Hunters

Fished only | Fished and hunted | Hunted only

Fishing and Hunting

This Survey reports information about residents of the United States who fished or hunted in 2011, regardless of whether they were licensed. The fishing and hunting sections report information for three groups: (1) sportspersons, (2) anglers, and (3) hunters.

Sportspersons

Sportspersons are those who fished or hunted. Individuals who fished or hunted commercially in 2011 are reported as sportspersons *only* if they also fished or hunted for recreation. The sportspersons group is composed of the three subgroups shown in the diagram below: (1) those that fished and hunted, (2) those that only fished, and (3) those that only hunted.

The total number of sportspersons is equal to the sum of people who only fished, only hunted, and both hunted and fished. It is not the sum of all anglers and all hunters because those people who both fished and hunted are included in both the angler and hunter population and would be incorrectly counted twice.

Anglers

Anglers are sportspersons who only fished plus those who fished and hunted. Anglers include not only licensed hook and line anglers, but also those who have no license and those who use special methods such as fishing with spears. Three types of fishing are reported: (1) freshwater, excluding the Great Lakes, (2) Great Lakes, and (3) saltwater. Since many anglers participated in more than one type of fishing, the total number of anglers is less than the sum of the three types of fishing.

Hunters

Hunters are sportspersons who only hunted plus those who hunted and fished. Hunters include not only licensed hunters using rifles and shotguns, but also those who have no license and those who engage in hunting with archery equipment, muzzleloaders, other primitive firearms, or pistols or handguns.

Four types of hunting are reported: (1) big game, (2) small game, (3) migratory bird, and (4) other animals. Since many hunters participated in more than one type of hunting, the sum of hunters for big game, small game, migratory bird, and other animals exceeds the total number of hunters.

Wildlife Watchers

Since 1980, the National Survey has included information on wildlife-watching activities in addition to fishing and hunting. However, unlike the 1980 and 1985 Surveys, the National Surveys since 1991 have collected data only for those activities where the *primary* purpose was wildlife watching (observing, photographing, or feeding wildlife).

The 2011 Survey uses a strict definition of wildlife watching. Participants must either take a "special interest" in wildlife around their homes or take a trip for the "primary purpose" of wildlife watching. Secondary wildlife watching, such as incidentally observing wildlife while pleasure driving, is not included.

Two types of wildlife-watching activity are reported: (1) away-from-home (formerly nonresidential) activities and (2) around-the-home (formerly residential) activities. Because some people participated in more than one type of wildlife watching, the sum of participants in each type will be greater than the total number of wildlife watchers. Only those engaged in activities whose *primary* purpose was wildlife watching are included in the Survey. The two types of wildlife-watching activity are defined below.

Away-From-Home

This group includes persons who took trips or outings of at least 1 mile from home for the primary purpose of observing, feeding, or photographing fish and wildlife. Trips to fish or hunt or scout and trips to zoos, circuses, aquariums, and museums are not considered wildlife-watching activities.

Around-The-Home

This group includes those who participated within 1 mile of home and involves one or more of the following: (1) closely observing or trying to identify birds or other wildlife; (2) photographing wildlife; (3) feeding birds or other wildlife; (4) maintaining natural areas of at least 1/4 acre where benefit to wildlife is the primary concern; (5) maintaining plantings (shrubs, agricultural crops, etc.) where benefit to wildlife is the primary concern; or (6) visiting parks and natural areas within 1 mile of home for the primary purpose of observing, feeding, or photographing wildlife.

2011 Indiana Summary

Activities in Indiana by Residents and Nonresidents

Fishing

Anglers	**801,000**
Days of fishing	20,775,000
Average days per angler	26
Total expenditures	$671,840,000
Trip-related	$427,310,000
Equipment and other	$244,530,000
Average per angler	$820
Average trip expenditure per day	$21

Hunting

Hunters	**392,000**
Days of hunting	10,863,000
Average days per hunter	28
Total expenditures	$222,310,000
Trip-related	$64,900,000
Equipment and other	$157,410,000
Average per hunter	$503
Average trip expenditure per day	$6

Wildlife Watching

Total wildlife-watching participants	**1,719,000**
Away-from-home participants	413,000
Around-the-home participants	1,657,000
Days of participation away from home	2,924,000
Average days of participation away from home	7
Total expenditures	$751,343,000
Trip-related	$206,357,000
Equipment and other	$544,985,000
Average per participant	$404
Average trip expenditure per day	$71

Activities by Indiana Residents Both Inside and Outside Indiana

Fishing

Anglers	**786,000**
Days of fishing	21,502,000
Average days per angler	27
Total expenditures	$649,164,000
Trip-related	$414,490,000
Equipment and other	$234,674,000
Average per angler	$826
Average trip expenditure per day	$19

Hunting

Hunters	**377,000**
Days of hunting	10,902,000
Average days per hunter	29
Total expenditures	$209,736,000
Trip-related	$57,014,000
Equipment and other	$152,722,000
Average per hunter	$556
Average trip expenditure per day	$5

Wildlife Watching

Total wildlife-watching participants	**1,681,000**
Away-from-home participants	477,000
Around-the-home participants	1,657,000
Days of participation away from home	3,552,000
Average days of participation away from home	7
Total expenditures	$1,003,303,000
Trip-related	$404,132,000
Equipment and other	$599,171,000
Average per participant	$597
Average trip expenditure per day	$114

Wildlife-Related Recreation

Participation in Indiana

The 2011 Survey found that 2.3 million Indiana residents and nonresidents 16 years old and older fished, hunted, or wildlife watched in Indiana. Of the total number of participants, 801 thousand fished, 392 thousand hunted, and 1.7 million participated in wildlife-watching activities, which includes observing, feeding, and photographing wildlife. The sum of anglers, hunters, and wildlife watchers exceeds the total number of participants in wildlife-related recreation because many of the individuals engaged in more than one wildlife-related activity.

Participation in 2011 by 6- to 15-Year-Old Indiana Residents

The focus of the National Survey is on the activity of participants 16 years old and older. However, the activity of 6- to 15-year-olds can be calculated using the screening data covering the year 2010. It is assumed for estimation purposes that the proportion of 6- to 15-year-old

participants to participants 16 years old and older remained the same in 2010 and 2011. Based on this assumption, in addition to the 786 thousand resident anglers 16 years old or older in Indiana, there were 301 thousand resident anglers 6 to 15 years old. Also, there were 377 thousand Hoosiers 16 years old and older and 46 thousand Hoosiers 6 to 15 years old who hunted. Finally, there were 1.7 million Hoosiers 16 years old and older and 375 thousand Hoosiers 6 to 15 years old who wildlife watched. Information on 2010 data for 6- to 15-year-olds is provided in Appendix B.

Expenditures in Indiana

In 2011, state residents and nonresidents spent $1.7 billion on wildlife recreation in Indiana. Of that total, trip-related expenditures were $699 million and equipment expenditures totaled $786 million. The remaining $208 million was spent on licenses, contributions, land ownership and leasing, and other items.

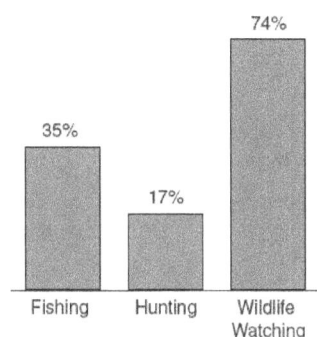

Percent of Total Participants by Activity
(Total: 2.3 million participants)

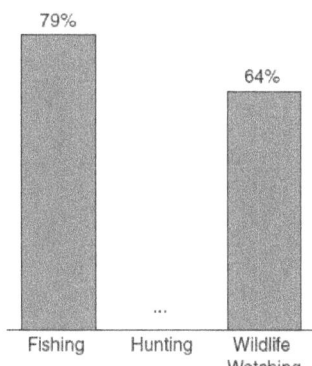

Percent of Total Residential Participants 6 to 15 Years Old by Activity: 2010
(Total: 540 thousand participants)

... Sample size too small (less than 10) to report data reliably.

Participants in Wildlife-Related Recreation in Indiana: 2011
(U.S. residents 16 years old and older)

Total	**2.3 million**
Sportspersons	
Total	**867 thousand**
Anglers.....................................	801 thousand
Hunters.....................................	392 thousand
Wildlife Watchers	
Total	**1.7 million**
Away from home	413 thousand
Around the home	1.7 million

Note: Detail does not add to total because of multiple responses

Source: Tables 1 and 24

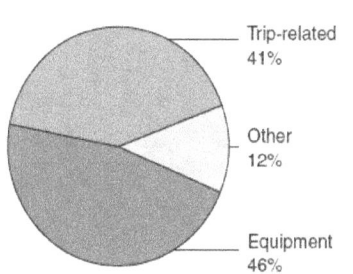

Wildlife-Related Recreation Expenditures in Inidana
(Total: $1.7 billion)

Sportspersons

In 2011, 867 thousand state resident and nonresident sportspersons 16 years old and older fished or hunted in Indiana. This group was comprised of 801 thousand anglers (92 percent of all sportspersons) and 392 thousand hunters (45 percent of all sportspersons). Among the 867 thousand sportspersons who fished or hunted in the state, 475 thousand (55 percent) fished but did not hunt in Indiana. Another 66 thousand (8 percent) hunted but did not fish there. The remaining 325 thousand (38 percent) fished and hunted in Indiana in 2011.

Sportspersons' Participation in Indiana
(State residents and nonresidents 16 years old and older)

Sportspersons (fished or hunted)	**867 thousand**
Anglers	**801 thousand**
Fished only	475 thousand
Fished and hunted	325 thousand
Hunters.	**392 thousand**
Hunted only	66 thousand
Hunted and fished.	325 thousand

Note: Detail does not add to total because of multiple responses

Source: Table 1

Anglers

Participants and Days of Fishing

In 2011, 801 thousand state residents and nonresidents 16 years old and older fished in Indiana. Of this total, 720 thousand anglers (90 percent) were state residents and 81 anglers (10 percent) were nonresidents. Anglers fished a total of 20.8 million days in Indiana—an average of 26 days per angler. State residents fished 20.2 million days—97 percent of all fishing days in Indiana. Nonresidents fished 537 thousand days in Indiana—3 percent of all fishing days in the state.

A large majority of Indiana residents who fished anywhere in the United States did so in their resident state. There were 786 thousand Indiana residents 16 years old and older who fished in the United States in 2011 for a total of 21.5 million days. An estimated 92 percent of all Indiana residents who fished did so in their home state. Of all fishing days by Indiana residents, 94 percent or 20.2 million were in their home state. For further details about fishing in Indiana, see Table 3.

Anglers in Indiana
(State residents and nonresidents 16 years old and older)

Anglers	**801 thousand**
Residents	720 thousand
Nonresidents	81 thousand
Days of fishing	**20.8 million**
Residents	20.2 million
Nonresidents	537 thousand

Source: Table 3

In State/Out of State
(State residents 16 years old and older)

Indiana anglers	**786 thousand**
In Indiana	720 thousand
In other states	166 thousand
Days of fishing	**21.5 million**
In Indiana	20.2 million
In other states	1.3 million

Note: Detail does not add to total because of multiple responses
Source: Table 3

Fishing Expenditures in Indiana

All fishing-related expenditures in Indiana totaled $672 million in 2011. Trip-related expenditures, including food and lodging, transportation, and other expenses totaled $427 million—64 percent of all fishing expenditures. Expenditures for food and lodging were $140 million and transportation expenditures were $137 million. Other trip expenses, such as equipment rental, bait, and cooking fuel, totaled $150 million. Each angler spent an average of $527 on trip-related costs during 2011.

Anglers spent $165 million on equipment in Indiana in 2011, 24 percent of all fishing expenditures. Fishing equipment (rods, reels, lines, etc.) spending totaled $92 million—56 percent of the equipment total. Auxiliary equipment expenditures (tents, special fishing clothing, etc.) and special equipment expenditures (boats, vans, etc.) amounted to $72 million—44 percent of the equipment total. Expenditures classified as special and auxiliary equipment are on items that were purchased for fishing but could be used in activities other than fishing.

The purchase of other items, such as magazines, membership dues, licenses, permits, stamps, and land leasing and ownership, amounted to $80 million—12 percent of all fishing expenditures. For more details about fishing expenditures in Indiana, see Tables 19 and 21 through 23.

Fishing Expenditures in Indiana
(State residents and nonresidents 16 years old and older)

Total	**$672 million**
Trip-related	$427 million
Equipment	$165 million
Fishing	$92 million
Auxiliary and special	$72 million
Other	$80 million

Source: Table 19

Fishing Expenditures in Indiana
(Total: $672 million)

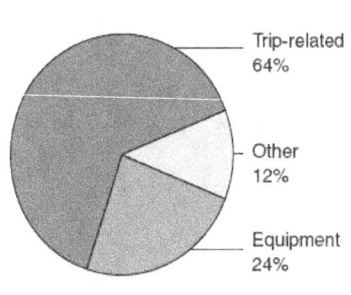

Trip-related 64%
Other 12%
Equipment 24%

Percent of Anglers by Residence
(Total: 801 thousand participants)

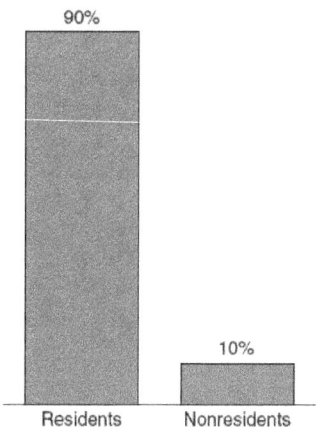

Residents 90%
Nonresidents 10%

Hunters

Participants and Days of Hunting

In 2011, there were 392 thousand residents and nonresidents 16 years old and older who hunted in Indiana. Resident hunters numbered 377 thousand, accounting for 96 percent of the hunters in Indiana. Residents and nonresidents hunted 10.9 million days in 2011, an average of 28 days per hunter. Residents hunted 10.8 million days in Indiana or 100 percent of all hunting days.

There were 377 thousand Indiana residents 16 years old and older who hunted in the United States in 2011 for a total of 10.9 million days. An estimated 100 percent of all Indiana residents who hunted did so in their home state. Of all hunting days by Indiana residents, 99 percent or 10.8 million were spent pursuing game in their home state. For further information on hunting activities by Indiana residents, see Table 3.

Hunters in Indiana
(State residents and nonresidents 16 years old and older)

Hunters	**392 thousand**
Residents	377 thousand
Nonresidents	...
Days of hunting	**10.9 million**
Residents	10.8 million
Nonresidents	...

... Sample size too small (less than 10) to report data reliably
Source: Table 3

In State/Out of State
(State residents 16 years old and older)

Indiana hunters	**377 thousand**
In Indiana	377 thousand
In other states	...
Days of hunting	**10.9 million**
In Indiana	10.8 million
In other states	...

... Sample size too small (less than 10) to report data reliably
Note: Detail does not add to total because of multiple responses
Source: Table 3

Hunting Expenditures in Indiana

All hunting-related expenditures in Indiana totaled $222 million in 2011. Trip-related expenses, such as food and lodging, transportation, and other trip expenses, totaled $65 million—29 percent of total expenditures. Expenditures for food and lodging were $26 million and transportation expenditures were $35 million. The average trip-related expenditure per hunter was $166.

Hunters spent $105 million on equipment—47 percent of all hunting expenditures. Hunting equipment (guns, ammunition, etc.) totaled $87 million and made up 83 percent of all equipment costs. Hunters spent $18 million on auxiliary equipment (tents, special hunting clothes, etc.) and special equipment (boats, vans, etc.), accounting for 17 percent of total equipment expenditures for hunting. Expenditures classified as special and auxiliary equipment are on items that were purchased for hunting but could be used in activities other than hunting.

The purchase of other items, such as magazines, membership dues, licenses, permits, and land leasing, and ownership, cost hunters $52 million—24 percent of all hunting expenditures. For more details on hunting expenditures in Indiana, see Tables 20 through 23.

Hunting Expenditures in Indiana
(State residents and nonresidents 16 years old and older)

Total	**$222 million**
Trip-related	$65 million
Equipment	$105 million
Hunting	$87 million
Auxiliary and special	$18 million
Other	$52 million

Source: Table 20

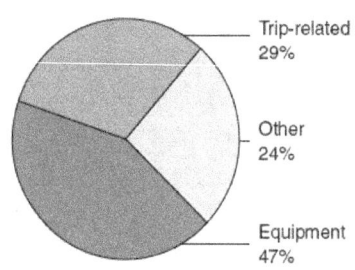

Hunting Expenditures in Indiana
(Total: $222 million)

Trip-related 29%

Other 24%

Equipment 47%

Comparative Hunting Expenditures by Type of Hunting

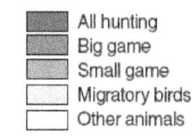

- All hunting
- Big game
- Small game
- Migratory birds
- Other animals

Trip expenditures per hunter:

$166 $136 $146 ... ...

Trip expenditures per day:

$11 $6 $6 ... ...

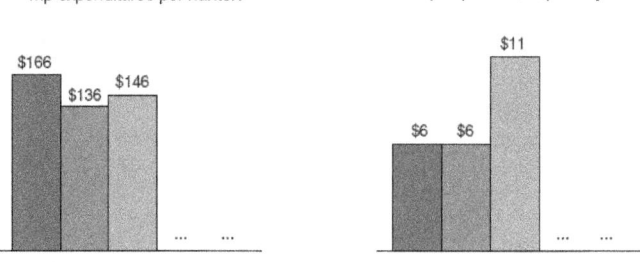

... Sample size too small (less than 10) to report data reliably.

Wildlife Watchers

Participants and Days of Activity

In 2011, 1.7 million U.S. residents 16 years old and older fed, observed, or photographed wildlife in Indiana. Most of them, 96 percent (1.7 million), enjoyed their activities close to home and are called "around-the-home" participants. Those persons who enjoyed wildlife at least one mile from home are called "away-from-home" participants. People participating in away-from-home activities in Indiana in 2011 numbered 413 thousand—24 percent of all wildlife watchers in Indiana. Of the 413 thousand, 375 thousand were state residents.

Hoosiers 16 years old and older who enjoyed away-from-home wildlife watching within their state totaled 375 thousand. Of this group, 251 thousand participants observed wildlife and 179 thousand photographed wildlife. Since some individuals engaged in more than one of the away-from-home activities during the year, the sum of wildlife observers, feeders, and photographers exceeds the total number away-from-home participants.

Hoosiers spent 2.7 million days engaged in away-from-home wildlife-watching activities in their state. They spent 2.1 million days observing and 1.2 million days photographing wildlife. For further details about away-from-home activities, see Table 25.

Indiana residents also took an active interest in wildlife around their homes. In 2011, 1.7 million state residents enjoyed observing, feeding, and photographing wildlife within one mile of their homes. Among this around-the-home group, 1.4 million fed, 1.2 million observed, and 407 thousand photographed wildlife around their homes. Another 239 thousand participants maintained natural areas of one-quarter acre or more for wildlife; 255 thousand participants maintained plantings for the benefit of wildlife; and 237 thousand participants visited parks or natural areas within a mile of home because of the wildlife. Summing the number of participants in these six activities results in an estimate that exceeds the total number of around-the-home participants because many people participated in more than one type of around-the-home activity. In addition, 27 percent of Hoosier around-the-home wildlife watchers also enjoyed wildlife away from home. For further details about Indiana residents participating in around-the-home wildlife-watching activities, see Table 27.

Wildlife-Watching Participants in Indiana
(State residents and nonresidents 16 years old and older)

Total	1.7 million
Around the home	1.7 million
Away from home	413 thousand

Note: Detail does not add to total because of multiple responses
Source: Table 24

Away-From-Home Wildlife-Watching Participation in Indiana
(State residents and nonresidents 16 years old and older)

Participants, total	413 thousand
Observe wildlife	266 thousand
Photograph wildlife	211 thousand
Feed wildlife	...
Days, total	2.9 million
Observe wildlife	2.2 million
Photograph wildlife	1.4 million
Feed wildlife	...

... Sample size too small (less than 10) to report data reliably
Note: Detail does not add to total because of multiple responses
Source: Table 25

Around-The-Home Wildlife-Watching Participation in Indiana
(State residents 16 years old and older)

Total	1.7 million
Feed wildlife	1.4 million
Observe wildlife	1.2 million
Photograph wildlife	407 thousand
Maintain natural areas	239 thousand
Maintain plantings	255 thousand
Visit parks and natural areas	237 thousand

Note: Detail does not add to total because of multiple responses
Source: Table 27

Wild Bird Observers

Bird watching attracted many wildlife enthusiasts in Indiana. In 2011, 1.2 million people observed birds around the home and on trips in the state. A majority, 96 percent (1.1 million), observed wild birds around the home while 22 percent (253 thousand) took trips away from home to watch birds.

Wildlife-Watching Expenditures in Indiana

Wildlife watchers spent $751 million on wildlife-watching activities in Indiana in 2011. Trip-related expenditures, including food and lodging ($76 million), transportation ($106 million), and other trip expenses ($25 million), such as equipment rental, amounted to $206 million. This summation comprised 27 percent of all wildlife-watching expenditures by participants. The average of the trip-related expenditures for away-from-home participants was $403 per person in 2011.

Wildlife-watching participants spent nearly $478 million on equipment—64 percent of all their expenditures. Specifically, wildlife-watching equipment (binoculars, special clothing, etc.) expenditures totaled $311 million, 65 percent of the equipment total. Auxiliary equipment expenditures (tents, backpacking equipment, etc.) and special equipment expenditures (campers, trucks, etc.) amounted to $167 million—35 percent of all equipment costs. Expenditures classified as special and auxiliary equipment are on items that were purchased for wildlife-watching recreation but could be used in activities other than wildlife watching.

Other items purchased by wildlife-watching participants, such as magazines, membership dues and contributions, land leasing and ownership, and plantings, totaled $67 million—9 percent of all wildlife-watching expenditures. For more details about wildlife-watching expenditures in Indiana, see Table 31.

Wild Bird Observers in Indiana
(State residents and nonresidents 16 years old and older)

Participants, total	**1.2 million**
Around the home	1.1 million
Away from home	253 thousand
Days, total	**143.2 million**
Around the home	141.1 million
Away from home	2.1 million

Note: Detail does not add to total because of multiple responses

Source: Table 29

Wildlife-Watching Expenditures in Indiana
(State residents and nonresidents 16 years old and older)

Total	**$751 million**
Trip-related	$206 million
Equipment	$478 million
Wildlife watching	$311 million
Auxiliary and special	$167 million
Other	$67 million

Source: Table 31

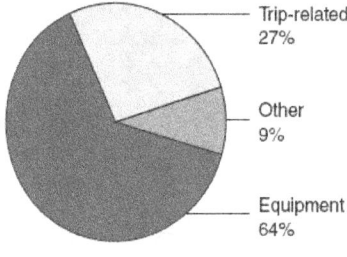

Wildlife-Watching Expenditures in Indiana (Total: $751 million)

Trip-related 27%
Other 9%
Equipment 64%

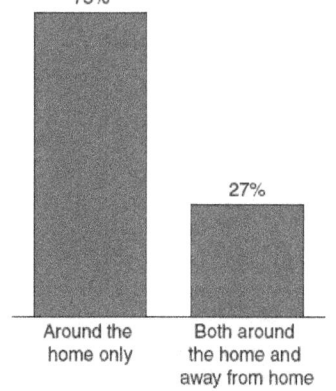

Away-From-Home Activity by Around-The-Home Participants (Total: 1.7 million participants)

Around the home only 73%
Both around the home and away from home 27%

2001–2011 Comparison

Comparing the estimates from the 2001, 2006, and 2011 Surveys gives a perspective on the state of wildlife-related recreation in the early twenty-first century in Indiana. Only the most general recreation comparisons are presented here.

The best way to compare estimates from surveys is not to compare the estimates themselves but to compare the confidence intervals around the esti-

mates. A 90-percent confidence interval around the estimate gives the range of estimates that 90 percent of all possible representative samples would supply. If the 90-percent confidence intervals of the two surveys' estimates overlap, it is not possible to say the two estimates are statistically different.

The state resident estimates cover the participation and expenditure activity of Indiana residents anywhere in the

United States. The in-state estimates cover the participation, day, and expenditure activity if U.S. residents in Indiana.

The expenditure estimates were made comparable by adjusting the estimates for inflation—all estimates are in 2011 dollars.

Indiana 2001 and 2011 Comparison
(Numbers in thousands. Expenditures in 2011 dollars)

	2001	2011	Percent change
Fishing			
Anglers in state	874	801	NS−8
Days in state	14,192	20,775	NS46
In-state expenditures by U.S. anglers	$659,020	$671,840	NS2
State resident anglers	833	786	NS−6
Total expenditures by state residents	$596,170	$649,164	NS9
Hunting			
Hunters in state	290	392	NS35
Days in state	5,000	10,863	NS117
In-state expenditures by U.S. hunters	$336,776	$222,310	NS−34
State resident hunters	284	377	NS33
Total expenditures by state residents	$355,216	$209,736	NS−41
Away-From-Home Wildlife Watching			
Participants in state	474	413	NS−13
Days in state	11,999	2,924	−76
State resident participants	484	477	NS−1
Around-The-Home Wildlife Watching			
Total participants	1,727	1,657	NS−4
Observers	1,295	1,180	NS−9
Feeders	1,615	1,394	NS−14
Wildlife-Watching Expenditures			
In-state expenditures by U.S. wildlife watchers	$916,854	$751,343	NS−18
Total expenditures by state residents	$774,381	$1,003,303	NS30

NS Not different from zero at the 10 percent level of significance

Indiana 2006 and 2011 Comparison
(Numbers in thousands. Expenditures in 2011 dollars)

	2006	2011	Percent change
Fishing			
Anglers in state	768	801	NS4
Days in state	9,805	20,775	112
In-state expenditures by U.S. anglers	$699,773	$671,840	NS−4
State resident anglers	739	786	NS6
Total expenditures by state residents	$777,009	$649,164	NS−16
Hunting			
Hunters in state	272	392	NS44
Days in state	4,808	10,863	NS126
In-state expenditures by U.S. hunters	$248,842	$222,310	NS−11
State resident hunters	254	377	48
Total expenditures by state residents	$271,197	$209,736	NS−23
Away-From-Home Wildlife Watching			
Participants in state	755	413	−45
Days in state	24,013	2,924	−88
State resident participants	611	477	NS−22
Around-The-Home Wildlife Watching			
Total participants	1,786	1,657	NS−7
Observers	1,092	1,180	NS8
Feeders	1,578	1,394	NS−12
Wildlife-Watching Expenditures			
In-state expenditures by U.S. wildlife watchers . . .	$1,042,039	$751,343	NS−28
Total expenditures by state residents	$1,246,628	$1,003,303	NS−20

NS Not different from zero at the 10 percent level of significance

---

Number of People Who Hunted and Fished in Indiana: 2001–2011
(In thousands)

Legend: Anglers, Hunters

Number of People Who Wildlife Watched in Indiana: 2001–2011
(In thousands)

Legend: Around the home, Away from home

Total Expenditures by Participants in Indiana
(In millions of 2011 dollars)

Legend: Anglers, Hunters, Wildlife Watchers

Tables

Guide to Statistical Tables

Purpose and Coverage of Tables

The statistical tables of this report were designed to meet a wide range of needs for those interested in wildlife-related recreation. Special terms used in these tables are defined in Appendix A.

The tables are based on responses to the 2011 Survey, which was designed to collect data about participation in wildlife-related recreation. To have taken part in the Survey, a respondent must have been a U.S. resident (a resident of one of the 50 states or the District of Columbia). No one residing outside the United States (including U.S. citizens) was eligible for interviewing. Therefore, reported state and national totals do not include participation by those who were not U.S. residents or who were U.S. citizens residing outside the United States.

Comparability With Previous Surveys

The numbers reported can be compared with those in the 1991, 1996, 2001, and 2006 Survey Reports. The methodology used in 2011 was similar to that used in those Surveys. These results should not be directly compared to results from Surveys earlier than 1991 since there were major changes in methodology. These changes were made to improve accuracy in the information provided.

Coverage of an Individual Table

Since the Survey covers many activities in various places by participants of different ages, all table titles, headnotes, stubs, and footnotes are designed to identify and articulate each item being reported in the table. For example, the title of Table 2 shows that data about anglers and hunters, their days of participation, and their number of trips are reported by type of activity. By contrast, the title of Table 7 indicates that it contains data on freshwater anglers and the days they fished for different species.

Percentages Reported in the Tables

Percentages are reported in the tables for the convenience of the user. When exclusive groups are being reported, the base of a percentage is apparent from its context because the percents add to 100 percent (plus or minus a rounding error). For example, Table 2 reports the number of trips taken by big game hunters, those taken by small game hunters, those taken by migratory bird hunters, and those taken by hunters pursuing other animals. These comprise 100 percent because they are exclusive categories.

Percents should not add to 100 when nonexclusive groups are being reported. Using Table 2 as an example again, note that adding the percentages associated with the total number of big game hunters, total small game hunters, total migratory bird hunters, and total hunters of other animals will not yield total hunters because respondents could hunt for more than one type of game.

When the base of the percentage is not apparent in context, it is identified in a footnote. For example, Table 15 reports two percentages with different bases: one base being the number of total participants at the head of the column and the other base being the total population who are described by the row category. Footnotes are used to clarify the bases of the reported percentages.

Footnotes to the Tables

Footnotes are used to clarify the information or items that are being reported in a table. Symbols in the body of a table indicate important footnotes. The following symbols are used in the tables to refer to the same footnote each time they appear:

*   Estimate based on a sample size of 10–29.

... Sample size too small to report data reliably.

Z   Less than 0.5 percent.

X   Not applicable.

NA Not available.

Estimates based upon fewer than ten responses are regarded as being based on a sample size that is too small for reliable reporting. An estimate based upon at least 10 but fewer than 30 responses is treated as an estimate based on a small sample size. Other footnotes appear, as necessary, to qualify or clarify the estimates reported in the tables. In addition, these two important footnotes appear frequently:

• Detail does not add to total because of multiple responses.

• Detail does not add to total because of multiple responses and nonresponse.

"Multiple responses" is a term used to reflect the fact that individuals or their characteristics fall into more than one category. Using Table 5 as an example, those who fished in saltwater and freshwater appear in both of these totals. Yet each angler is represented only once in the "Total, all fishing" row. Similarly, in Table 12, those who hunt for big game and small game are counted only once as a hunter in the "Total, all hunting" row. Therefore, totals will be smaller than the sum of subcategories when multiple responses exist.

"Nonresponse" exists because the Survey questions were answered voluntarily, and some respondents did not or could not answer all the questions.

Table 1. Fishing and Hunting in Indiana by Resident and Nonresident Sportspersons: 2011

(Population 16 years old and older. Numbers in thousands)

Sportspersons	Total, state residents and nonresidents		State residents		Nonresidents	
	Number	Percent of sportspersons	Number	Percent of resident sportspersons	Number	Percent of nonresident sportspersons
Total sportspersons (fished or hunted)	867	100	776	100	*91	*100
Total anglers	801	92	720	93	*81	*88
Fished only	475	55	399	51		
Fished and hunted	325	38	322	41		
Total hunters	392	45	377	49	...	...
Hunted only	*66	*8	*56	*7		
Hunted and fished	325	38	322	41		

* Estimate based on a sample size of 10–29   ... Sample size too small (less than 10) to report data reliably

Note: Detail does not add to total because of multiple responses

Table 2. Anglers and Hunters, Days of Participation, and Trips in Indiana by Type of Fishing and Hunting: 2011

(Population 16 years old and older. Numbers in thousands)

Type of fishing and hunting	Participants		Days of participation		Trips	
	Number	Percent	Number	Percent	Number	Percent
FISHING						
Total, all fishing.........................	801	100	20,775	100	15,878	100
Total, all freshwater	726	91	19,438	94	15,878	100
Freshwater, except Great Lakes	716	89	19,324	93	15,828	100
Great Lakes						
Saltwater	(X)	(X)	(X)	(X)	(X)	(X)
HUNTING						
Total, all hunting.........................	392	100	10,863	100	8,912	100
Big game	266	68	6,261	58	5,855	66
Small game	*126	*32	*1,666	*15	*1,795	*20
Migratory birds						
Other animals						

* Estimate based on a sample size of 10–29   ... Sample size too small (less than 10) to report data reliably   (X) Not applicable

Note: Detail does not add to total because of multiple responses

Table 3. Anglers and Hunters, Trips, and Days of Participation: 2011

(Population 16 years old and older. Numbers in thousands)

Anglers and hunters, trips and days of participation	Activity in Indiana						Activity by Indiana residents in United States					
	Total, state residents and nonresidents		State residents		Nonresidents		Total, in state of residence and in other states		In state of residence		In other states	
	Number	Percent	Number	Percent	Number	Percent	Number	Percent	Number	Percent	Number	Percent
FISHING												
Total anglers	801	100	720	90	*81	*10	786	100	720	92	*166	*21
Total trips	15,878	100	15,429	97	*449	*3	16,318	100	15,429	95	*889	*5
Total days of fishing	20,775	100	20,238	97	*537	*3	21,502	100	20,238	94	*1,304	*6
Average days of fishing	26	(X)	28	(X)	*7	(X)	27	(X)	28	(X)	*8	(X)
HUNTING												
Total hunters	392	100	377	96			377	100	377	100		
Total trips	8,912	100	8,863	99			8,952	100	8,863	99		
Total days of hunting	10,863	100	10,814	100			10,902	100	10,814	99		
Average days of hunting	28	(X)	29	(X)		(X)	29	(X)	29	(X)		(X)

* Estimate based on a sample size of 10–29   … Sample size too small (less than 10) to report data reliably   (X) Not applicable

Note: Detail does not add to total because of multiple responses

Table 4. Indiana Resident Anglers and Hunters by Place Fished or Hunted: 2011

(Population 16 years old and older. Numbers in thousands)

Place fished or hunted	Anglers		Hunters	
	Number	Percent	Number	Percent
Total, all places	**786**	**100**	**377**	**100**
In-state only	620	79	360	96
In-state and other states	*100	*13		
In other states only				

* Estimate based on a sample size of 10–29   … Sample size too small (less than 10) to report data reliably

Note: Detail does not add to total because of multiple responses and nonresponse

Table 5. Indiana Resident Anglers and Hunters, Days of Participation, and Trips in the United States by Type of Fishing and Hunting: 2011

(Population 16 years old and older. Numbers in thousands)

Type of fishing and hunting	Participants		Days of participation		Trips	
	Number	Percent	Number	Percent	Number	Percent
FISHING						
Total, all fishing	**786**	**100**	**21,502**	**100**	**16,318**	**100**
Total, all freshwater	711	90	20,273	94	16,245	100
Freshwater, except Great Lakes	702	89	20,096	93	16,171	99
Great Lakes						
Saltwater						
HUNTING						
Total, all hunting	**377**	**100**	**10,902**	**100**	**8,952**	**100**
Big game	269	71	6,299	58	5,863	65
Small game	*126	*33	*1,720	*16	*1,861	*21
Migratory birds						
Other animals						

* Estimate based on a sample size of 10–29   … Sample size too small (less than 10) to report data reliably

Note: Detail does not add to total because of multiple responses

Table 6. Freshwater Anglers, Trips, Days of Fishing, and Type of Water Fished: 2011

(Population 16 years old and older. Numbers in thousands)

Anglers, trips, and days of fishing	Activity in Indiana					
	Total, state residents and nonresidents		State residents		Nonresidents	
	Number	Percent	Number	Percent	Number	Percent
Total anglers	716	100	636	89	*81	*11
Total trips...	15,828	100	15,383	97	*445	*3
Total days of fishing	19,324	100	18,787	97	*537	*3
Average days of fishing	27	(X)	30	(X)	*7	(X)
ANGLERS						
Total, all types of water..............................	716	100	636	89	*81	*11
Ponds, lakes, or reservoirs	659	100	582	88		
Rivers or streams	185	100	185	100		
DAYS						
Total, all types of water..............................	19,324	100	18,787	97	*537	*3
Ponds, lakes, or reservoirs	15,561	100	15,043	97		
Rivers or streams	4,824	100	4,824	100		

* Estimate based on a sample size of 10–29   ... Sample size too small (less than 10) to report data reliably   (X) Not applicable

Note: Detail does not add to total because of multiple responses

Table 7. Freshwater Anglers and Days of Fishing in Indiana by Type of Fish: 2011

(Population 16 years old and older. Numbers in thousands)

Anglers and days of fishing	Activity in Indiana						
	Total, state residents and nonresidents			State residents		Nonresidents	
	Number	Percent of total types	Percent of anglers/days	Number	Percent of anglers/days	Number	Percent of anglers/days
ANGLERS							
Total, all types of fish	716	100	100	636	89	*81	*11
Crappie	269	37	100	256	95		
Panfish	454	63	100	393	87		
White bass, striped bass, striped bass hybrids	*206	*29	*100	*178	*87		
Black bass	346	48	100	319	92		
Catfish, bullheads	188	26	100	*160	*85		
Walleye, sauger							
Northern pike, pickerel, muskie, muskie hybrids							
Steelhead							
Trout							
Salmon							
Anything[1]							
Other freshwater fish							
DAYS							
Total, all types of fish	19,324	100	100	18,787	97	*537	*3
Crappie	7,167	37	100	6,893	96		
Panfish	8,986	47	100	8,644	96		
White bass, striped bass, striped bass hybrids	*4,355	*23	*100	*4,327	*99		
Black bass	10,659	55	100	10,322	97		
Catfish, bullheads	2,538	13	100	*2,255	*89		
Walleye, sauger							
Northern pike, pickerel, muskie, muskie hybrids							
Steelhead							
Trout							
Salmon							
Anything[1]							
Other freshwater fish							

* Estimate based on a sample size of 10–29   ... Sample size too small (less than 10) to report data reliably

[1] Respondent fished for no specific species and identified "Anything" from a list of categories of fish

Note: Detail does not add to total because of multiple responses

Table 8. Great Lakes Anglers, Trips, and Days of Fishing in Indiana: 2011

(Population 16 years old and older. Numbers in thousands)

Anglers, trips, and days of fishing	Activity in Indiana					
	Total, state residents and nonresidents		State residents		Nonresidents	
	Number	Percent	Number	Percent	Number	Percent
Total anglers	...	...	...	...	...	...
Total trips..	...	...	...	...	...	...
Total days...	...	...	...	...	...	...
Average days of fishing		(X)		(X)		(X)

... Sample size too small (less than 10) to report data reliably   (X) Not applicable

Table 9. Great Lakes Anglers and Days of Fishing in Indiana by Type of Fish: 2011

(Population 16 years old and older. Numbers in thousands)

Anglers and days of fishing	Activity in Indiana						
	Total, state residents and nonresidents			State residents		Nonresidents	
	Number	Percent of total types	Percent of anglers/days	Number	Percent of anglers/days	Number	Percent of anglers/days
ANGLERS							
Total, all types of fish	...	...	...	...	...	...	...
Perch							
Black bass							
Walleye, sauger							
Northern pike, pickerel, muskie, muskie hybrids							
Salmon							
Steelhead							
Lake trout							
Other trout							
Anything[1]							
Other Great Lakes fish							
DAYS							
Total, all types of fish	...	...	...	...	...	...	...
Perch							
Black bass							
Walleye, sauger							
Northern pike, pickerel, muskie, muskie hybrids							
Salmon							
Steelhead							
Lake trout							
Other trout							
Anything[1]							
Other Great Lakes fish							

... Sample size too small (less than 10) to report data reliably

[1] Respondent fished for no specific species and identified "Anything" from a list of categories of fish

Table 10. Saltwater Anglers, Trips, and Days of Fishing in Indiana: 2011

This table does not apply to this state.

Table 11. Saltwater Anglers and Days of Fishing in Indiana by Type of Fish: 2011

This table does not apply to this state.

Table 12. Hunters, Trips, and Days of Hunting in Indiana by Type of Hunting: 2011

(Population 16 years old and older. Numbers in thousands)

Hunters, trips, and days of hunting	Activity in Indiana					
	Total, state residents and nonresidents		State residents		Nonresidents	
	Number	Percent	Number	Percent	Number	Percent
HUNTERS						
Total, all hunting.........................	392	100	377	96	...	...
Big game	266	100	262	99		
Small game	*126	*100	*126	*100		
Migratory birds						
Other animals						
TRIPS						
Total, all hunting.........................	8,912	100	8,863	99	...	...
Big game	5,855	100	5,840	100		
Small game	*1,795	*100	*1,795	*100		
Migratory birds						
Other animals						
DAYS						
Total, all hunting.........................	10,863	100	10,814	100	...	...
Big game	6,261	100	6,245	100		
Small game	*1,666	*100	*1,666	*100		
Migratory birds						
Other animals						

* Estimate based on a sample size of 10–29   ... Sample size too small (less than 10) to report data reliably

Note: Detail does not add to total because of multiple responses

Table 13. Hunters and Days of Hunting in Indiana by Type of Game: 2011

(Population 16 years old and older. Numbers in thousands)

Type of game	Hunters, state residents and nonresidents		Days of hunting	
	Number	Percent	Number	Percent
Total, all types of game.....................	392	100	10,863	100
Big game, total.........................	266	68	6,261	58
Deer	266	68	5,372	49
Elk				
Bear				
Wild turkey	*80	*20	*281	*3
Other big game				
Small game, total.....................	*126	*32	*1,666	*15
Rabbit, hare	*98	*25	*730	*7
Quail				
Grouse/prairie chicken				
Squirrel	*84	*22	*1,050	*10
Pheasant				
Other small game				
Migratory birds, total....................	...	...	...	...
Waterfowl				
Geese				
Ducks				
Doves				
Other migratory birds				
Other animals, total[1].....................	...	...	...	...

* Estimate based on a sample size of 10–29   ... Sample size too small (less than 10) to report data reliably

[1] Includes groundhog, raccoon, fox, coyote, crow, prairie dog, etc

Note: Detail does not add to total because of multiple responses

Table 14. Hunters and Days of Hunting in Indiana by Type of Land: 2011

(Population 16 years old and older. Numbers in thousands)

Hunters and days of hunting	Total, state residents and nonresidents		State residents		Nonresidents	
	Number	Percent	Number	Percent	Number	Percent
HUNTERS						
Total, all types of land.....................	392	100	377	100	...	...
Public land, total.......................	*106	*27	*102	*27		
Public land only						
Public and private land	*95	*24	*95	*25		
Private land, total	376	96	366	97		
Private land only	281	72	270	72		
Private and public land	*95	*24	*95	*25		
DAYS						
Total, all types of land.....................	10,863	100	10,814	100	...	...
Public land[1]	*656	*6	*629	*6		
Private land[2]	8,725	80	8,704	80		

* Estimate based on a sample size of 10–29   ... Sample size too small (less than 10) to report data reliably

[1] Days of hunting on public land includes both days spent solely on public land and those spent on public and private land

[2] Days of hunting on private land includes both days spent solely on private land and those spent on private and public land

Note: Detail does not add to total because of multiple responses and nonresponse

Table 15. Selected Characteristics of Indiana Resident Anglers and Hunters: 2011

(Population 16 years old and older. Numbers in thousands)

Characteristic	Population		Sportspersons (fished or hunted)			Anglers			Hunters		
	Number	Percent	Number	Percent who par-ticipated	Percent of sports-persons	Number	Percent who par-ticipated	Percent of anglers	Number	Percent who par-ticipated	Percent of hunters
Total persons	4,965	100	842	17	100	786	16	100	377	8	100
Population Density of Residence											
Urban	3,533	71	476	13	57	456	13	58	*172	*5	*46
Rural	1,432	29	366	26	43	330	23	42	205	14	54
Population Size of Residence											
Metropolitan Statistical Area (MSA)	4,614	93	796	17	95	741	16	94	343	7	91
1,000,000 or more	2,123	43	302	14	36	294	14	37	*64	*3	*17
250,000 to 999,999	773	16	*73	*9	*9						
50,000 to 249,999	1,719	35	421	25	50	398	23	51	244	14	65
Outside MSA	351	7									
Sex											
Male	2,363	48	720	30	86	664	28	84	374	16	99
Female	2,602	52	*122	*5	*14	*122	*5	*16			
Age											
16 to 17 years	*78	*2									
18 to 24 years	533	11	*66	*12	*8	*66	*12	*8			
25 to 34 years	665	13	*187	*28	*22	*180	*27	*23			
35 to 44 years	829	17	163	20	19	150	18	19	*52	*6	*14
45 to 54 years	1,129	23	136	12	16	*120	*11	*15	*52	*5	*14
55 to 64 years	892	18	*139	*16	*17	*121	*14	*15			
65 years and older	839	17	*129	*15	*15	*129	*15	*16			
65 to 74 years	478	10	*121	*25	*14	*121	*25	*15			
75 and older	362	7									
Ethnicity											
Hispanic	*253	*5									
Non-Hispanic	4,713	95	840	18	100	784	17	100	377	8	100
Race											
White	4,164	84	756	18	90	700	17	89	377	9	100
African American	577	12									
All others	*224	*5									
Annual Household Income											
Less than $20,000	553	11									
$20,000 to $29,999	411	8	*48	*12	*6	*48	*12	*6			
$30,000 to $39,999	634	13	*127	*20	*15	*116	*18	*15			
$40,000 to $49,999	372	7									
$50,000 to $74,999	949	19	165	17	20	*148	*16	*19	*93	*10	*25
$75,000 to $99,999	482	10	*157	*33	*19	*150	*31	*19			
$100,000 to $149,999	286	6	*70	*25	*8	*61	*21	*8			
$150,000 or more	111	2									
Not reported	1,167	24	*166	*14	*20	*155	*13	*20			
Education											
11 years or less	433	9	*58	*13	*7	*58	*13	*7			
12 years	2,772	56	464	17	55	425	15	54	257	9	68
1 to 3 years of college	913	18	*131	*14	*16	*121	*13	*15	*52	*6	*14
4 years or more of college	847	17	189	22	22	183	22	23	*50	*6	*13

* Estimate based on a sample size of 10–29   ... Sample size too small (less than 10) to report data reliably

Note: Detail does not add to total because of multiple responses Percent who participated columns show the percent of each row's population who participated in the activity named by the column (the percent of those living in urban areas who fished, etc) Remaining percent columns show the percent of each column's participants who are described by the row heading (the percent of anglers who lived in urban areas, etc)

Table 16. Summary of Expenditures in Indiana by State Residents and Nonresidents Combined for Fishing and Hunting: 2011

(Population 16 years old and older)

Expenditure item	Amount (thousands of dollars)	Spenders (thousands)	Average per spender (dollars)[1]	Average per sportsperson (dollars)[1]
FISHING AND HUNTING				
Total	**941,286**	**1,035**	**909**	**1,043**
Food and lodging	165,827	514	323	191
Transportation	172,351	584	295	193
Other trip costs[2]	154,032	545	282	178
Equipment (fishing, hunting)	182,883	733	249	184
Auxiliary equipment[3]	37,991	183	208	41
Special equipment[4]	*86,775	*79	*1,092	*100
Magazines, books, and DVDs	*8,511	*238	*36	*10
Membership dues and contributions	*12,230	*201	*61	*13
Other[5]	120,686	600	201	133
FISHING				
Total	**671,840**	**910**	**738**	**820**
Food and lodging	140,320	441	318	175
Transportation	136,879	497	276	165
Other trip costs[2]	150,110	537	280	187
Fishing equipment	92,066	626	147	107
Auxiliary equipment[3]	*12,805	*80	*160	*14
Special equipment[4]				
Magazines, books, and DVDs	*5,167	*146	*35	*6
Membership dues and contributions				
Other[5]	72,938	481	152	88
HUNTING				
Total	**222,310**	**455**	**489**	**503**
Food and lodging	25,507	233	109	65
Transportation	35,471	268	132	91
Other trip costs[2]				
Hunting equipment	86,825	317	274	169
Auxiliary equipment[3]	*15,676	*74	*212	*38
Special equipment[4]				
Magazines, books, and DVDs				
Membership dues and contributions				
Other[5]	47,748	245	195	115
UNSPECIFIED[6]				
Total	***42,780**	***144**	***297**	***49**

* Estimate based on a sample size of 10–29 ... Sample size too small (less than 10) to report data reliably

[1] Average expenditures are annual estimates

[2] Includes boating costs, equipment rental, guide fees, access fees, heating and cooking fuel, and ice and bait (for fishing only)

[3] Includes sleeping bags, packs, duffel bags, tents, binoculars and field glasses, special fishing and hunting clothing, foul weather gear, boots and waders, maintenance and repair of equipment, processing and taxidermy costs, and electronic equipment such as a GPS device

[4] Includes big-ticket items bought primarily for hunting and fishing including boats, campers, cabins, trail bikes, dune buggies, 4 x 4 vehicles, ATVs, 4-wheelers, snowmobiles, pickups, vans, travel and tent trailers, motor homes, house trailers, recreational vehicles (RVs) and other special equipment

[5] Includes land leasing and ownership, licenses, stamps, tags, permits, and plantings (for hunting only)

[6] Respondent could not specify whether expenditure was primarily for either fishing or hunting

Note: Detail does not add to total because of multiple responses and nonresponse

Table 17. Summary of Fishing Trip and Equipment Expenditures in Indiana by State Residents and Nonresidents Combined by Type of Fishing: 2011

(Population 16 years old and older)

Expenditure item	Amount (thousands of dollars)	Spenders (thousands)	Average per spender (dollars)[1]	Average per angler (dollars)[1]
ALL FISHING				
Total	**591,826**	**797**	**742**	**723**
Food and lodging	140,320	441	318	175
Transportation	136,879	497	276	165
Other trip costs	150,110	537	280	187
Equipment	164,516	646	255	195
ALL FRESHWATER				
Total	**573,057**	**726**	**789**	**701**
Food and lodging	140,320	441	318	175
Transportation	135,831	497	273	165
Other trip costs	150,110	537	280	187
Equipment	146,795	565	260	173
FRESHWATER, EXCEPT GREAT LAKES				
Total	**569,623**	**717**	**795**	**696**
Food and lodging	139,341	432	322	174
Transportation	135,124	487	277	164
Other trip costs	148,692	528	282	186
Equipment	146,466	561	261	173
GREAT LAKES				
Total	...	...	...	...
Food and lodging				
Transportation				
Other trip costs				
Equipment				
SALTWATER				
Total	...	...	...	...
Food and lodging				
Transportation				
Other trip costs				
Equipment				

... Sample size too small (less than 10) to report data reliably

[1] Average expenditures are annual estimates

Note: Detail does not add to total because of multiple responses and nonresponse See Table 19 for detailed listing of expenditure items

Table 18. Summary of Hunting Trip and Equipment Expenditures in Indiana by State Residents and Nonresidents Combined by Type of Hunting: 2011

(Population 16 years old and older)

Expenditure item	Amount (thousands of dollars)	Spenders (thousands)	Average per spender (dollars)[1]	Average per type of hunter (dollars)[1]
ALL HUNTING				
Total	**169,908**	**404**	**421**	**379**
Food and lodging	25,507	233	109	65
Transportation	35,471	268	132	91
Other trip costs				
Equipment	105,008	338	311	213
BIG GAME				
Total	**88,899**	**260**	**342**	**225**
Food and lodging	*13,932	*142	*98	*36
Transportation	*19,711	*162	*122	*50
Other trip costs				
Equipment	52,650	205	257	133
SMALL GAME				
Total	***40,490**	***137**	***295**	***153**
Food and lodging	*6,788	*80	*85	*34
Transportation	*10,343	*121	*86	*51
Other trip costs				
Equipment	*22,044	*94	*233	*62
MIGRATORY BIRDS				
Total	...	...	...	...
Food and lodging				
Transportation				
Other trip costs				
Equipment				
OTHER ANIMALS				
Total	...	...	...	...
Food and lodging				
Transportation				
Other trip costs				
Equipment				

* Estimate based on a sample size of 10–29   ... Sample size too small (less than 10) to report data reliably

[1] Average expenditures are annual estimates

Note: Detail does not add to total because of multiple responses and nonresponse See Table 20 for detailed listing of expenditure items

Table 19. Expenditures in Indiana by State Residents and Nonresidents Combined for Fishing: 2011

(Population 16 years old and older)

Expenditure item	Expenditures		Spenders		
	Amount (thousands of dollars)	Average per angler (dollars)[1]	Number (thousands)	Percent of anglers	Average per spender (dollars)[1]
Total, all items	**671,840**	**820**	**910**	**114**	**738**
TRIP-RELATED EXPENDITURES					
Total trip-related	427,310	527	617	77	692
Food and lodging, total	140,320	175	441	55	318
Food	96,087	120	438	55	219
Lodging	*44,233	*55	*58	*7	*759
Transportation	136,879	165	497	62	276
Other trip costs, total	150,110	187	537	67	280
Privilege and other fees[2]	*10,951	*14	*139	*17	*79
Boating costs[3]	*83,310	*104	*191	*24	*436
Bait	49,734	62	446	56	111
Ice	5,207	7	259	32	20
Heating and cooking fuel					
EQUIPMENT AND OTHER EXPENDITURES PRIMARILY FOR FISHING					
Fishing equipment, total	92,066	107	626	78	147
Reels, rods, and rod-making components	39,403	47	298	37	132
Lines, hooks, sinkers, etc	17,886	19	547	68	33
Artificial lures and flies	21,564	25	471	59	46
Creels, stringers, fish bags, landing nets, and gaff hooks	*2,256		*144	*18	*16
Minnow seines, traps, and bait containers					
Other fishing equipment[4]	*10,031	*12	*180	*22	*56
Auxiliary equipment[5]	*12,805	*14	*80	*10	*160
Special equipment[6]					
Other fishing costs[7]	80,015	97	522	65	153

* Estimate based on a sample size of 10–29   ... Sample size too small (less than 10) to report data reliably

[1] Average expenditures are annual estimates

[2] Includes boat or equipment rental and fees for guides, pack trip (party and charter boats, etc), public land use, and private land use

[3] Includes boat launching, mooring, storage, maintenance, insurance, pumpout fees, and fuel

[4] Includes electronic fishing devices (depth finders, fish finders, etc), tackle boxes, ice fishing equipment, and other fishing equipment

[5] Includes sleeping bags, packs, duffel bags, tents, binoculars and field glasses, special fishing clothing, foul weather gear, boots and waders, maintenance and repair of equipment, processing and taxidermy costs, and electronic equipment such as a GPS device

[6] Includes big-ticket items bought primarily for fishing including boats, campers, cabins, trail bikes, dune buggies, 4 x 4 vehicles, ATVs, 4-wheelers, snowmobiles, pickups, vans, travel and tent trailers, motor homes, house trailers, recreational vehicles (RVs) and other special equipment

[7] Includes magazines, books, and DVDs, membership dues and contributions, land leasing and ownership, and licenses, stamps, tags, and permits

Note: Detail does not add to total because of multiple responses and nonresponse   Percent of anglers may be greater than 100 because spenders who did not fish in this state are included

Table 20. Expenditures in Indiana by State Residents and Nonresidents Combined for Hunting: 2011

(Population 16 years old and older)

Expenditure item	Expenditures		Spenders		
	Amount (thousands of dollars)	Average per hunter (dollars)[1]	Number (thousands)	Percent of hunters	Average per spender (dollars)[1]
Total, all items	**222,310**	**503**	**455**	**116**	**489**
TRIP-RELATED EXPENDITURES					
Total trip-related	**64,900**	**166**	**297**	**76**	**219**
Food and lodging, total	**25,507**	**65**	**233**	**59**	**109**
Food	24,790	63	233	59	106
Lodging					
Transportation	35,471	91	268	69	132
Other trip costs, total	...	...	...	...	...
Privilege and other fees[2]					
Boating costs[3]					
Heating and cooking fuel					
EQUIPMENT AND OTHER EXPENDITURES PRIMARILY FOR HUNTING					
Hunting equipment, total	**86,825**	**169**	**317**	**81**	**274**
Firearms					
Ammunition	10,765	27	244	62	44
Other hunting equipment[4]	54,159	*95	185	47	292
Auxiliary equipment[5]	*15,676	*38	*74	*19	*212
Special equipment[6]					
Other hunting costs[7]	52,402	125	335	85	157

* Estimate based on a sample size of 10–29   ... Sample size too small (less than 10) to report data reliably

[1] Average expenditures are annual estimates

[2] Includes guide fees, pack trip and package fees, public and private land use access fees, and rental of equipment such as boats and hunting or camping equipment

[3] Boating costs include launching, mooring, storage, maintenance, insurance, pumpout fees, and fuel

[4] Includes telescopic sights, decoys and game calls, handloading equipment and components, hunting dogs and associated costs, hunting knives, bows, arrows, archery equipment, and other hunting equipment

[5] Includes sleeping bags, packs, duffel bags, tents, binoculars and field glasses, special hunting clothing, foul weather gear, boots and waders, maintenance and repair of equipment, processing and taxidermy costs, and electronic equipment such as a GPS device

[6] Includes big-ticket items bought primarily for hunting including boats, campers, cabins, trail bikes, dune buggies, 4 x 4 vehicles, ATVs, 4-wheelers, snowmobiles, pickups, vans, travel and tent trailers, motor homes, house trailers, recreational vehicles (RVs) and other special equipment

[7] Includes magazines, books, and DVDs, membership dues and contributions, land leasing and ownership, and licenses, stamps, tags, and permits

Note: Detail does not add to total because of multiple responses and nonresponse Percent of hunters may be greater than 100 because spenders who did not hunt in this state are included

Table 21. Trip and Equipment Expenditures in Indiana for Fishing and Hunting by Indiana Residents and Nonresidents: 2011

(Population 16 years old and older)

Expenditure item	Amount (thousands of dollars)	Spenders (thousands)	Average per spender (dollars)[1]	Average per sportsperson (dollars)[1]
STATE RESIDENTS AND NONRESIDENTS				
Trip and equipment expenditures for fishing and hunting, total	799,858	900	888	2,042
Trip and equipment expenditures for fishing, total	591,868	800	740	723
Food and lodging	140,320	441	318	175
Transportation	136,879	497	276	165
Boating costs[2]	*83,310	*191	*436	*104
Other trip costs[3]	66,801	518	129	83
Equipment	164,558	648	254	195
Trip and equipment expenditures for hunting, total	174,009	430	404	379
Food and lodging	25,507	233	109	65
Transportation	35,471	268	132	91
Boating costs[2]				
Other trip costs[3]				
Equipment	109,110	365	299	213
Unspecified equipment[4]	*33,981	*50	*680	*87
STATE RESIDENTS				
Trip and equipment expenditures for fishing and hunting, total	682,489	782	873	1,810
Trip and equipment expenditures for fishing, total	502,884	718	701	684
Food and lodging	83,513	408	205	116
Transportation	128,775	451	285	172
Boating costs[2]	*80,992	*175	*463	*112
Other trip costs[3]	60,898	489	125	85
Equipment	148,706	587	253	199
Trip and equipment expenditures for hunting, total	146,018	371	393	377
Food and lodging	25,202	218	115	67
Transportation	34,414	254	136	91
Boating costs[2]				
Other trip costs[3]				
Equipment	82,481	316	261	208
Unspecified equipment[4]	*33,587	*46	*730	*89
NONRESIDENTS				
Trip and equipment expenditures for fishing and hunting, total	*117,370	*119	*990	...
Trip and equipment expenditures for fishing, total	*88,984	*82	*1,088	...
Food and lodging				
Transportation				
Boating costs[2]				
Other trip costs[3]				
Equipment	*15,852	*61	*259	
Trip and equipment expenditures for hunting, total	*27,991	*59	*475	...
Food and lodging				
Transportation				
Boating costs[2]				
Other trip costs[3]				
Equipment				
Unspecified equipment[4]	...	...	...	...

* Estimate based on a sample size of 10–29   ... Sample size too small (less than 10) to report data reliably

[1] Average expenditures are annual estimates

[2] Includes boat launching, mooring, storage, maintenance, insurance, pumpout fees, and fuel

[3] Includes equipment rental, guide and access fees, ice and bait for fishing, and heating and cooking oil

[4] Respondent could not specify whether item was for hunting or fishing

Note: Detail does not add to total because of multiple responses and nonresponse

Table 22. Summary of Indiana Residents' Fishing and Hunting Expenditures Both Inside and Outside Indiana: 2011

(Population 16 years old and older)

Expenditure item	Amount (thousands of dollars)	Spenders (thousands)	Average per spender (dollars)[1]	Average per sportsperson (dollars)[1]
FISHING AND HUNTING				
Total	907,443	814	1,115	1,078
Food and lodging	143,777	538	267	171
Transportation	176,644	585	302	210
Other trip costs[2]	155,004	541	286	184
Equipment (fishing, hunting)	181,916	665	273	216
Auxiliary equipment[3]	46,870	185	254	56
Special equipment[4]	*75,761	*68	*1,107	*90
Magazines, books, and DVDs	*8,730	*244	*36	*10
Membership dues and contributions	*12,645	*194	*65	*15
Other[5]	106,095	573	185	126
FISHING				
Total	649,164	757	858	826
Food and lodging	118,575	485	244	151
Transportation	144,832	515	281	184
Other trip costs[2]	151,083	533	283	192
Fishing equipment	100,310	587	171	128
Auxiliary equipment[3]	*21,410	*89	*240	*27
Special equipment[4]				
Magazines, books, and DVDs	*5,293	*150	*35	*7
Membership dues and contributions				
Other[5]	57,120	476	120	73
HUNTING				
Total	209,736	368	569	556
Food and lodging	25,202	218	115	67
Transportation	31,812	254	125	84
Other trip costs[2]				
Hunting equipment	77,172	280	275	205
Auxiliary equipment[3]	*15,650	*63	*250	*42
Special equipment[4]				
Magazines, books, and DVDs				
Membership dues and contributions				
Other[5]	48,975	239	205	130
UNSPECIFIED[6]				
Total	*42,983	*137	*315	*51

* Estimate based on a sample size of 10–29   ... Sample size too small (less than 10) to report data reliably

[1] Average expenditures are annual estimates

[2] Includes boating costs, equipment rental, guide fees, access fees, heating and cooking fuel, and ice and bait (for fishing only)

[3] Includes sleeping bags, packs, duffel bags, tents, binoculars and field glasses, special fishing and hunting clothing, foul weather gear, boots and waders, maintenance and repair of equipment, processing and taxidermy costs, and electronic equipment such as a GPS device

[4] Includes big-ticket items bought primarily for hunting and fishing including boats, campers, cabins, trail bikes, dune buggies, 4 x 4 vehicles, ATVs, 4-wheelers, snowmobiles, pickups, vans, travel and tent trailers, motor homes, house trailers, recreational vehicles (RVs) and other special equipment

[5] Includes land leasing and ownership, licenses, stamps, tags, and permits, and plantings (for hunting only)

[6] Respondent could not specify whether expenditure was primarily for fishing or hunting

Note: Detail does not add to total because of multiple responses and nonresponse See Tables 19–20 for a detailed listing of expenditure items

Table 23. In-State and Out-of-State Expenditures by Indiana Residents for Fishing and Hunting: 2011

(State population 16 years old and older)

Expenditure item	Amount (thousands of dollars)	Spenders (thousands)	Average per spender (dollars)[1]	Average per sportsperson (dollars)[1]
IN INDIANA				
Expenditures for fishing and hunting, total	**800,425**	**804**	**996**	**923**
Trip-related expenditures	417,716	634	659	482
Equipment (fishing and hunting)	154,456	663	233	178
Auxiliary equipment[2]	34,555	162	214	40
Special equipment[3]	*75,761	*68	*1,107	*87
Other[4]	117,936	584	202	136
Expenditures for fishing, total	**563,568**	**757**	**745**	**704**
Trip-related expenditures	354,178	568	624	442
Fishing equipment	89,296	583	153	112
Auxiliary equipment[2]	*10,736	*69	*155	*13
Special equipment[3]				
Other[4]	60,726	430	141	76
Expenditures for hunting, total	**190,722**	**368**	**518**	**487**
Trip-related expenditures	63,538	282	225	162
Hunting equipment	61,330	280	219	157
Auxiliary equipment[2]	*14,704	*60	*246	*38
Special equipment[3]				
Other[4]	48,642	302	161	124
Unspecified expenditures for fishing and hunting, total[5]	***41,943**	***124**	***339**	***48**
OUT OF STATE				
Expenditures for fishing and hunting, total	**162,945**	**735**	**222**	**188**
Trip-related expenditures	*113,636	*167	*679	*131
Equipment (fishing and hunting)	*27,460	*665	*41	*32
Auxiliary equipment[2]				
Special equipment[3]				
Other[4]	*9,534	*433	*22	*11
Expenditures for fishing, total	***110,665**	***622**	***178**	***138**
Trip-related expenditures	*85,380	*162	*528	*107
Fishing equipment				
Auxiliary equipment[2]				
Special equipment[3]				
Other[4]	*3,597	*306	*12	*4
Expenditures for hunting, total	***50,480**	***316**	***160**	***129**
Trip-related expenditures				
Hunting equipment				
Auxiliary equipment[2]				
Special equipment[3]				
Other[4]				
Unspecified expenditures for fishing and hunting, total[5]	...	...	...	...

* Estimate based on a sample size of 10–29   ... Sample size too small (less than 10) to report data reliably

[1] Average expenditures are annual estimates

[2] Auxiliary equipment includes sleeping bags, packs, duffel bags, tents, binoculars and field glasses, special fishing and hunting clothing, foul weather gear, boots and waders, maintenance and repair of equipment, processing and taxidermy costs, and electronic equipment such as a GPS device

[3] Special equipment includes boats, campers, cabins, trail bikes, dune buggies, 4 x 4 vehicles, ATVs, 4-wheelers, snowmobiles, pickups, vans, travel and tent trailers, motor homes, house trailers, recreational vehicles (RVs) and other special equipment

[4] Other equipment includes expenditures for magazines, books, DVDs, membership dues and contributions, land leasing and ownership, licenses, stamps, tags, and permits, and plantings

[5] Respondent could not specify whether expenditure was primarily for either fishing or hunting

Note: Detail does not add to total because of multiple responses and nonresponse

Table 24. Wildlife Watching in Indiana by State Residents and Nonresidents Combined: 2011

(Population 16 years old and older. Numbers in thousands)

Participants	Number	Percent
Total participants	**1,719**	**100**
Away from home	*413	*24
Observe wildlife	*266	*15
Photograph wildlife	*211	*12
Feed wildlife		
Around the home	1,657	96
Observe wildlife	1,180	69
Photograph wildlife	407	24
Feed wildlife	1,394	81
Visit parks or natural areas[1]	*237	*14
Maintain plantings or natural areas	433	25

* Estimate based on a sample size of 10–29   ... Sample size too small (less than 10) to report data reliably

[1] Includes visits only to parks or natural areas within one mile of home

Note: Detail does not add to total because of multiple responses

Table 25. Participants, Trips, and Days of Participation in Away-From-Home Wildlife Watching in Indiana: 2011

(Population 16 years old and older. Numbers in thousands)

Participants, trips, and days of participation	Activity in Indiana					
	Total, state residents and nonresidents		State residents		Nonresidents	
	Number	Percent	Number	Percent	Number	Percent
PARTICIPANTS						
Total participants	*413	*100	*375	*100	...	...
Observe wildlife	*266	*64	*251	*67		
Photograph wildlife	*211	*51	*179	*48		
Feed wildlife						
TRIPS						
Total Trips	*2,650	*100	*2,571	*100	...	...
Average days per trip	*1	(X)	*1	(X)		(X)
DAYS						
Total days	*2,924	*100	*2,743	*100	...	...
Observing wildlife	*2,180	*75	*2,139	*78		
Photographing wildlife	*1,390	*48	*1,234	*45		
Feeding wildlife						
Average days per participant	*7	(X)	*7	(X)	...	(X)
Observing wildlife	*8	(X)	*9	(X)		(X)
Photographing wildlife	*7	(X)	*7	(X)		(X)
Feeding wildlife		(X)		(X)		(X)

* Estimate based on a sample size of 10–29   ... Sample size too small (less than 10) to report data reliably   (X) Not applicable

Note: Detail does not add to total because of multiple responses and nonresponse

Table 26. Away-From-Home Wildlife-Watching Participants by Wildlife Observed, Photographed, or Fed in Indiana: 2011

(Population 16 years old and older. Numbers in thousands)

Wildlife observed, photographed, or fed	Total, state residents and nonresidents		State residents		Nonresidents	
	Number	Percent	Number	Percent	Number	Percent
Total all wildlife.................................	*413	*100	*375	*91	...	...
Total birds..	*268	*100	*254	*94	...	...
Songbirds (cardinals, robins, warblers, etc)	*235	*100	*220	*94		
Birds of prey (hawks, owls, eagles, etc)	*147	*100	*132	*90		
Waterfowl (ducks, geese, swans, etc)	*264	*100	*249	*94		
Other water birds (shorebirds, herons, cranes, etc)	*194	*100	*194	*100		
Other birds (pheasants, turkeys, road runners, etc)	*89	*100	*89	*100		
Total land mammals...............................	*243	*100	*211	*87	...	...
Large land mammals (bears, bison, elk, etc)	*179	*100	*179	*100		
Small land mammals (prairie dogs, squirrels, etc)	*123	*100	*91	*74		
Fish (salmon, sharks, etc)						
Marine mammals (whales, dolphins, etc)						
Other wildlife (butterflies, turtles, etc)	*189	*100	*180	*95		

* Estimate based on a sample size of 10–29   ... Sample size too small (less than 10) to report data reliably

Note: Detail does not add to total because of multiple responses

Table 27. Participation in Wildlife-Watching Activities Around the Home in Indiana: 2011

(State population 16 years old and older. Numbers in thousands)

Around the home	Participants	
	Number	Percent
Total around-the-home participants....................................	1,657	100
Observe wildlife	1,180	71
Visit parks and natural areas[1]	*237	*14
Photograph wildlife	407	25
Feed wildlife	1,394	84
Maintain natural areas	*239	*14
Maintain plantings	*255	*15
Participants Observing Wildlife		
Total, all wildlife	**1,180**	**100**
Birds	1,124	95
Land mammals	1,039	88
Large mammals	627	53
Small mammals	971	82
Amphibians or reptiles	*413	*35
Insects or spiders	*568	*48
Fish and other wildlife	*273	*23
Total, 1 day or more	**1,180**	**100**
1 to 10 days	*114	*10
11 to 50 days	*490	*42
51 to 200 days	*144	*12
201 days or more	416	35
Participants Visiting Parks or Natural Areas[1]		
Total, 1 day or more	***237**	***100**
1 to 5 days		
6 to 10 days		
11 days or more		
Participants Photographing Wildlife		
Total, 1 day or more	**407**	**100**
1 to 3 days	*135	*33
4 to 10 days	*141	*35
11 or more days	*130	*32
Participants Feeding Wildlife		
Total, all wildlife	**1,394**	**100**
Wild birds	1,357	97
Other wildlife	691	50

* Estimate based on a sample size of 10–29   ... Sample size too small (less than 10) to report data reliably

[1] Includes visits only to parks or natural areas within one mile of home

Note: Detail does not add to total because of multiple responses and nonresponse

Table 28. Indiana Residents Participating in Wildlife Watching in the United States: 2011

(State population 16 years old and older Numbers in thousands)

Participants	Number	Percent of participants	Percent of population
Total participants	**1,681**	**100**	**34**
Away from home	477	28	10
Around the home	1,657	99	33
Observe wildlife	1,180	70	24
Photograph wildlife	407	24	8
Feed wild birds or other wildlife	1,394	83	28
Maintain plantings or natural areas	433	26	9
Visit parks or natural areas[1]	*237	*14	*5

* Estimate based on a sample size of 10–29

[1] Includes visits to publicly or privately owned parks or natural areas

Note: Detail does not add to total because of multiple responses The column showing percent of participants is based on total participants The column showing percent of population is based on the state population 16 years old and older, including those who did not participate in wildlife watching

Table 29. Wild Bird Observers and Days of Observation in Indiana by State Residents and Nonresidents: 2011

(Population 16 years old and older. Numbers in thousands)

Observers and days of observation	Total, state residents and nonresidents		State residents		Nonresidents	
	Number	Percent	Number	Percent	Number	Percent
OBSERVERS						
Total bird observers	**1,175**	**100**	**1,160**	**100**	...	...
Around-the-home observers	1,124	96	1,124	97	(X)	(X)
Away-from-home observers	*253	*22	*239	*21		
DAYS						
Total days observing birds	**143,238**	**100**	**143,197**	**100**	...	...
Around the home	141,141	99	141,141	99	(X)	(X)
Away from home	*2,097	*1	*2,056	*1		

* Estimate based on a sample size of 10–29   ... Sample size too small (less than 10) to report data reliably   (X) Not applicable

Note: Detail does not add to total because of multiple responses

Table 30. Selected Characteristics of Indiana Residents Participating in Wildlife Watching: 2011

(State population 16 years old and older. Numbers in thousands)

Characteristic	Population		Participants Total			Away from home			Around the home		
	Number	Percent	Number	Percent who par-ticipated	Percent	Number	Percent who par-ticipated	Percent	Number	Percent who par-ticipated	Percent
Total persons	4,965	100	1,681	34	100	477	10	100	1,657	33	100
Population Density of Residence											
Urban	3,533	71	1,060	30	63	*395	*11	*83	1,040	29	63
Rural	1,432	29	621	43	37	*82	*6	*17	617	43	37
Population Size of Residence											
Metropolitan Statistical Area (MSA)	4,614	93	1,469	32	87	361	8	76	1,445	31	87
1,000,000 or more	2,123	43	615	29	37				615	29	37
250,000 to 999,999	773	16	*198	*26	*12				*190	*25	*11
50,000 to 249,999	1,719	35	656	38	39	*137	*8	*29	640	37	39
Outside MSA	351	7									
Sex											
Male	2,363	48	867	37	52	*356	*15	*74	859	36	52
Female	2,602	52	814	31	48	*122	*5	*26	798	31	48
Age											
16 to 17 years	*78	*2									
18 to 24 years	533	11									
25 to 34 years	665	13									
35 to 44 years	829	17	*248	*30	*15				*240	*29	*14
45 to 54 years	1,129	23	393	35	23	*173	*15	*36	377	33	23
55 to 64 years	892	18	353	40	21				353	40	21
65 years and older	839	17	509	61	30				509	61	31
65 to 74 years	478	10	*304	*64	*18				*304	*64	*18
75 and older	362	7	*205	*57	*12				*205	*57	*12
Ethnicity											
Hispanic	*253	*5									
Non-Hispanic	4,713	95	1,681	36	100	477	10	100	1,657	35	100
Race											
White	4,164	84	1,655	40	98	477	11	100	1,631	39	98
African American	577	12									
All others	*224	*5									
Annual Household Income											
Less than $20,000	553	11									
$20,000 to $29,999	411	8	*131	*32	*8				*131	*32	*8
$30,000 to $39,999	634	13	*197	*31	*12				*197	*31	*12
$40,000 to $49,999	372	7	*232	*62	*14				*227	*61	*14
$50,000 to $74,999	949	19	*298	*31	*18				*286	*30	*17
$75,000 to $99,999	482	10	*222	*46	*13	*127	*26	*27	*222	*46	*13
$100,000 to $149,999	286	6	*117	*41	*7				*117	*41	*7
$150,000 or more	111	2									
Not reported	1,167	24	*362	*31	*22				*354	*30	*21
Education											
11 years or less	433	9									
12 years	2,772	56	771	28	46	*202	*7	*42	767	28	46
1 to 3 years of college	913	18	*281	*31	*17				*273	*30	*16
4 years or more of college	847	17	552	65	33	*232	*27	*49	544	64	33

* Estimate based on a sample size of 10–29   ... Sample size too small (less than 10) to report data reliably

Note: Detail does not add to total because of multiple responses and nonresponse Percent who participated columns show the percent of each row's population who participated in the activity named by the column (the percent of those living in urban areas who participated, etc) Percent columns show the percent of each column's participants who are described by the row heading (the percent of those who participated who live in urban areas, etc)

(Population 16 years old and older)

Expenditure item	Expenditures (thousands of dollars)	Average per participant (dollars)[1]	Spenders		
			Number (thousands)	Percent of wildlife-watching participants[2]	Average per spender (dollars)[1]
Total, all items	751,343	404	1,474	86	510
TRIP EXPENDITURES					
Total, trip-related	*206,357	*403	*416	*101	*496
Food and lodging	*75,968	*184	*374	*91	*203
Food	*48,151	*117	*374	*91	*129
Lodging					
Transportation	*105,843	*159	*402	*97	*263
Other trip costs[3]	*24,546	*59	*343	*83	*72
EQUIPMENT AND OTHER EXPENDITURES					
Total	544,985	307	1,417	82	385
Wildlife-watching equipment, total	311,412	178	1,322	77	236
Binoculars, spotting scopes	*24,752	*14	*216	*13	*114
Film and photo processing					
Cameras, special lenses, video cameras, and other photographic equipment, including memory cards	*41,318	*24	*214	*12	*193
Day packs, carrying cases, and special clothing					
Bird food	144,360	83	1,049	61	138
Food for other wildlife	50,888	30	591	34	86
Nest boxes, bird houses, bird feeders, and bird baths	27,925	*16	532	31	53
Other equipment (including field guides)					
Auxiliary equipment[4]	*151,057	*88	*296	*17	*511
Special equipment[5]					
Magazines, books, and DVDs	*15,233	*9	*444	*26	*34
Membership dues and contributions	*21,386	*12	*260	*15	*82
Land leasing and ownership					
Plantings	*12,878	*7	*255	*15	*50

* Estimate based on a sample size of 10–29   ... Sample size too small (less than 10) to report data reliably

[1] Average expenditures are annual estimates

[2] Percent of wildlife-watching participants column for trip-related expenditures is based on away-from-home participation For equipment and other expenditures, the percent of wildlife-watching participants column is based on total wildlife-watching participants

[3] Includes equipment rental and fees for guides, pack trips, public land use and private land use, boat fuel, other boating costs, and heating and cooking fuel

[4] Includes tents, tarps, frame packs and other backpacking equipment, other camping equipment, and other auxiliary equipment

[5] Includes boats, campers, cabins, trail bikes, dune buggies, 4 x 4 vehicles, ATVs, 4-wheelers, snowmobiles, pickups, vans, travel and tent trailers, motor homes, house trailers, recreational vehicles (RVs) and other special equipment

Note: Detail does not add to total because of multiple responses and nonresponse

Table 32. Trip and Equipment Expenditures in Indiana for Wildlife Watching by Indiana Residents and Nonresidents: 2011

(Population 16 years old and older)

Expenditure item	Amount (thousands of dollars)	Spenders (thousands)	Average per spender (dollars)[1]	Average per participant (dollars)[1]
STATE RESIDENTS AND NONRESIDENTS				
Total	**684,557**	**1,409**	**486**	**365**
Food and lodging	*75,968	*374	*203	*184
Transportation	*105,843	*402	*263	*159
Other trip costs[2]	*24,546	*343	*72	*59
Equipment[3]	478,200	1,336	358	269
STATE RESIDENTS				
Total	**660,937**	**1,310**	**505**	**369**
Food and lodging	*72,052	*336	*214	*192
Transportation	*102,854	*364	*282	*168
Other trip costs[2]	*24,369	*311	*78	*65
Equipment[3]	461,663	1,274	362	275
NONRESIDENTS				
Total	...	...	...	...
Food and lodging				
Transportation				
Other trip costs[2]				
Equipment[3]				

* Estimate based on a sample size of 10–29   ... Sample size too small (less than 10) to report data reliably

[1] Average expenditures are annual estimates

[2] Includes equipment rental and fees for guides, pack trips, public land use, private land use, boat fuel, other boating costs, and heating and cooking fuel

[3] Includes wildlife-watching auxiliary and special equipment

Note: Detail does not add to total because of multiple responses and nonresponse See Table 33 for detailed listed of expenditure items

Table 33. Wildlife-Watching Expenditures Both Inside and Outside Indiana by Indiana Residents: 2011

(State population 16 years old and older)

Expenditure item	Expenditures (thousands of dollars)	Average per participant (dollars)[1]	Spenders		
			Number (thousands)	Percent of wildlife-watching participants[2]	Average per spender (dollars)[1]
Total, all items...	1,003,303	597	1,405	84	714
TRIP EXPENDITURES					
Total, trip-related	*404,132	*846	*408	*85	*990
Food and lodging	*193,651	*406	*402	*84	*482
Food	*58,076	*122	*391	*82	*148
Lodging	*135,575	*284	*306	*64	*444
Transportation	*183,635	*385	*395	*83	*465
Other trip costs[3]	*26,846	*56	*349	*73	*77
EQUIPMENT AND OTHER EXPENDITURES					
Total	599,171	356	1,373	82	436
Wildlife-watching equipment, total.........................	336,873	200	1,261	75	267
Binoculars, spotting scopes	*41,011	*24	*216	*13	*189
Film and photo processing					
Cameras, special lenses, video cameras, and other photographic equipment, including memory cards	*40,597	*24	*206	*12	*197
Day packs, carrying cases, and special clothing					
Bird food	146,263	87	1,035	62	141
Food for other wildlife	51,567	31	601	36	86
Nest boxes, bird houses, bird feeders, and bird baths	28,187	17	532	32	53
Other equipment					
Auxiliary equipment[4]	*154,889	*92	*330	*20	*469
Special equipment[5]					
Magazines, books, and DVDs	*15,830	*9	*452	*27	*35
Membership dues and contributions	*57,544	*34	*292	*17	*197
Land leasing and ownership					
Plantings	*12,878	*8	*255	*15	*50

* Estimate based on a sample size of 10–29   ... Sample size too small (less than 10) to report data reliably

[1] Average expenditures are annual estimates

[2] Percent of wildlife-watching participants column for trip-related expenditures is based on away-from-home participation. For equipment and other expenditures, the percent of wildlife-watching participants column is based on total wildlife-watching participants

[3] Includes equipment rental and fees for guides, pack trips, public land use and private land use, boat fuel, other boating costs, and heating and cooking fuel

[4] Includes tents, tarps, frame packs and other backpacking equipment, other camping equipment, and other auxiliary equipment

[5] Includes boats, campers, cabins, trail bikes, dune buggies, 4 x 4 vehicles, ATVs, 4-wheelers, snowmobiles, pickups, vans, travel and tent trailers, motor homes, house trailers, recreational vehicles (RVs) and other special equipment

Note: Detail does not add to total because of multiple responses and nonresponse

Table 34. In-State and Out-of-State Expenditures by Indiana Residents for Wildlife Watching: 2011

(State population 16 years old and older)

Expenditure Item	Amount (thousands of dollars)	Spenders (thousands)	Average per spender (dollars)[1]	Average per participant (dollars)[1]
IN INDIANA				
Expenditures for wildlife watching, total[2].................	**727,627**	**1,354**	**537**	**433**
Trip-related expenditures[3]	*199,274	*378	*527	*531
Wildlife-watching equipment[4]	306,737	1,261	243	182
Auxiliary equipment[5]	*151,057	*296	*511	*90
Special equipment[6]				
Other[7]	66,690	617	108	40
OUT OF STATE				
Expenditures for wildlife watching, total[2].................	***239,602**	***291**	***823**	***2,577**
Trip-related expenditures[3]	*204,858	*80	*2,567	*2,567
Wildlife-watching equipment[4]	*30,136	*211	*143	
Auxiliary equipment[5]				
Special equipment[6]				
Other[7]				

* Estimate based on a sample size of 10–29   ... Sample size too small (less than 10) to report data reliably

[1] Average expenditures are annual estimates

[2] Information on trip-related expenditures was collected for away-from-home participants only Equipment and other expenditures are based on information collected from both away-from-home and around-the-home participants

[3] Includes equipment rental and fees for guides, pack trips, public land use and private land use, boat fuel, other boating costs, and heating and cooking fuel

[4] Includes binoculars, spotting scopes, cameras, special lenses, videocameras, other photography equipment, memory cards, film and photo processing, commercially prepared and packaged wild bird food, other bulk food used to feed wild birds, food used to feed other wildlife, nest boxes, bird houses, feeders, baths, and other wildife-watching equipment

[5] Includes tents, tarps, frame packs and other backpacking equipment, other camping equipment, and other auxiliary equipment

[6] Includes boats, campers, cabins, trail bikes, dune buggies, 4 x 4 vehicles, ATVs, 4-wheelers, snowmobiles, pickups, vans, travel and tent trailers, motor homes, house trailers, recreational vehicles (RVs) and other special equipment

[7] Includes magazines, books, DVDs, membership dues and contributions, and land leasing and ownership

Note: Detail does not add to total because of multiple responses and nonresponse

Table 35. Participation of Indiana Resident Wildlife-Watching Participants in Fishing and Hunting: 2011

(State population 16 years old and older. Numbers in thousands)

Participants	Total wildlife watchers		Wildlife-watching activity			
			Away from home		Around the home	
	Number	Percent	Number	Percent	Number	Percent
Total participants	**1,681**	**100**	**477**	**100**	**1,657**	**100**
Wildlife-watching participants who:						
Did not fish or hunt	1,289	77	*331	*69	1,284	77
Fished or hunted	392	23	*147	*31	373	23
Fished	366	22	*137	*29	350	21
Hunted	218	13			215	13

* Estimate based on a sample size of 10–29   ... Sample size too small (less than 10) to report data reliably

Note: Detail does not add to total because of multiple responses and nonresponse

Table 36. Participation of Indiana Resident Sportspersons in Wildlife-Watching Activities: 2011

(State population 16 years old and older. Numbers in thousands)

Sportspersons	Sportspersons		Anglers		Hunters	
	Number	Percent	Number	Percent	Number	Percent
Total sportspersons..	842	100	786	100	377	100
Sportspersons who:						
Did not engage in wildlife-watching activities	450	53	420	53	*159	*42
Engaged in wildlife-watching activities	392	47	366	47	218	58
Away from home	*147	*17	*137	*17		
Around the home	373	44	350	44	215	57

* Estimate based on a sample size of 10–29   ... Sample size too small (less than 10) to report data reliably

Note: Detail does not add to total because of multiple responses and nonresponse

State reports for previous Surveys included tables that had estimates for all fifty states. In order to expedite release of the 2011 Indiana State report, state estimates have been deleted. To find state estimates other than Indiana, go to *http://wsfrprograms.fws.gov/Subpages/NationalSurvey/reports2011.html.* State reports are being released alphabetically, beginning in early 2013.

Appendix A

Appendix A.
Definitions

Annual household income—Total 2011 income of household members before taxes and other deductions.

Around-the-home wildlife watching—Activity within 1 mile of home with one of six primary purposes: (1) taking special interest in or trying to identify birds or other wildlife; (2) photographing wildlife; (3) feeding birds or other wildlife; (4) maintaining natural areas of at least one-quarter acre for the benefit of wildlife; (5) maintaining plantings (such as shrubs and agricultural crops) for the benefit of wildlife; and (6) visiting parks and natural areas to observe, photograph, or feed wildlife.

Auxiliary equipment—Equipment owned primarily for wildlife-associated recreation. For the sportspersons section, these include sleeping bags, packs, duffel bags, tents, binoculars and field glasses, special fishing and hunting clothing, foul weather gear, boots and waders, maintenance and repair of equipment, and processing and taxidermy costs. For the wildlife-watching section, these include tents, tarps, frame packs, backpacking and other camping equipment, and blinds. For both sportspersons and wildlife watchers, it also includes electronic auxiliary equipment such as Global Positioning Systems.

Away-from-home wildlife watching—Trips or outings at least 1 mile from home for the primary purpose of observing, photographing, or feeding wildlife. Trips to zoos, circuses, aquariums, and museums are not included.

Big game—Bear, deer, elk, moose, wild turkey, and similar large animals that are hunted.

Census Divisions

East North Central
Illinois
Indiana
Michigan
Ohio
Wisconsin

East South Central
Alabama
Kentucky
Mississippi
Tennessee

Middle Atlantic
New Jersey
New York
Pennsylvania

Mountain
Arizona
Colorado
Idaho
Montana
Nevada
New Mexico
Utah
Wyoming

New England
Connecticut
Maine
Massachusetts
New Hampshire
Rhode Island
Vermont

Pacific
Alaska
California
Hawaii
Oregon
Washington

South Atlantic
Delaware
District of Columbia
Florida
Georgia
Maryland
North Carolina
South Carolina
Virginia
West Virginia

West North Central
Kansas
Iowa
Minnesota
Missouri
Nebraska
North Dakota
South Dakota

West South Central
Arkansas
Louisiana
Oklahoma
Texas

Day—Any part of a day spent participating in a given activity. For example, if someone hunted two hours one day and three hours another day, it would be reported as two days of hunting. If someone hunted two hours in the morning and three hours in the afternoon of the same day, it would be considered one day of hunting.

Education—The highest completed grade of school or year of college.

Expenditures—Money spent in 2011 for wildlife-related recreation trips in the United States, wildlife-related recreational equipment purchased in the United States, and other items. The "other items" were books, magazines, and DVDs; membership dues and contributions, land leasing or owning; hunting and fishing licenses; and plantings, all for the purpose of wildlife-related recreation. Expenditures included both money spent by participants for themselves and the value of gifts they received.

Fishing—The sport of catching or attempting to catch fish with a hook and line, bow and arrow, or spear; it also includes catching or gathering shellfish (clams, crabs, etc.); and the noncommercial seining or netting of fish, unless the fish are for use as bait. For example, seining for smelt is fishing, but seining for bait minnows is not included as fishing.

Fishing equipment—Items owned primarily for fishing:

  Rods, reels, poles, and rodmaking components

  Lines and leaders

  Artificial lures, flies, baits, and dressing for flies or lines

  Hooks, sinkers, swivels, and other items attached to a line, except lures and baits

  Tackle boxes

  Creels, stringers, fish bags, landing nets, and gaff hooks

  Minnow traps, seines, and bait containers

  Depth finders, fish finders, and other electronic fishing devices

  Ice fishing equipment

  Other fishing equipment

Freshwater—Reservoirs, lakes, ponds, and the nontidal portions of rivers and streams.

Great Lakes fishing—Fishing in Lakes Superior, Michigan, Huron, St. Clair, Erie, and Ontario, their connecting waters such as the St. Mary's River system, Detroit River, St. Clair River, and the Niagara River, and the St. Lawrence River south of the bridge at Cornwall, New York. Great Lakes fishing includes fishing in tributaries of the Great Lakes for smelt, steelhead, and salmon.

Home—The starting point of a wildlife-related recreational trip. It may be a permanent residence or a temporary or seasonal residence such as a cabin.

Hunting—The sport of shooting or attempting to shoot wildlife with firearms or archery equipment.

Hunting equipment—Items owned primarily for hunting:

Rifles, shotguns, muzzleloaders, and handguns

Archery equipment

Telescopic sights

Decoys and game calls

Ammunition

Hand loading equipment

Hunting dogs and associated costs

Other hunting equipment

Land leasing and owning—Leasing or owning land either singly or in cooperation with others for the primary purpose of fishing, hunting, or wildlife watching on it.

Maintain natural areas—To set aside 1/4 acre or more of natural environment, such as wood lots or open fields, for the primary purpose of benefiting wildlife.

Maintain plantings—To introduce or encourage the growth of food and cover plants for the primary purpose of benefiting wildlife.

Metropolitan Statistical Area (MSA)—A Metropolitan Statistical Area is a grouping of one or more counties or equivalent entities that contain at least one urbanized area of 50,000 or more inhabitants. The "Outside MSA" classification include census-defined Micropolitan Statistical Areas (or Micro areas). A Micro area is defined as a grouping of one or more counties or equivalent entities that contain at least one urban cluster of at least 10,000 but less than 50,000 inhabitants. Refer to <www.census.gov /population/metro/about/>, for a more detailed definition of the Metropolitan Statistical Area.

Migratory birds—Birds that regularly migrate from one region or climate to another such as ducks, geese, and doves and other birds that may be hunted.

Multiple responses—The term used to reflect the fact that individuals or their characteristics fall into more than one reporting category. An example of a big game hunter who hunted for deer and elk demonstrates the effect of multiple responses. In this case, adding the number of deer hunters (one) and elk hunters (one) would overstate the number of big game hunters (one) because deer and elk hunters are not

mutually exclusive categories. In contrast, for example, total participants is the sum of male and female participants, because "male" and "female" are mutually exclusive categories.

Nonresidents—Individuals who do not live in the State being reported. For example, a person living in Texas who watches whales in California is a nonresidential wildlife-watcher in California.

Nonresponse—A term used to reflect the fact that some Survey respondents provide incomplete sets of information. For example, a Survey respondent may have been unable to identify the primary type of hunting for which a gun was bought. Total hunting expenditure estimates will include the gun purchase, but it will not appear as spending for big game or any other type of hunting. Nonresponses result in reported totals that are greater than the sum of their parts.

Observe—To take special interest in or try to identify birds, fish or other wildlife.

Other animals—Coyotes, crows, foxes, groundhogs, prairie dogs, raccoons, alligators, and similar animals that can be legally hunted and are not classified as big game, small game, or migratory birds. They may be classified as unprotected or predatory animals by the State in which they are hunted. Feral pigs are classified as "other animals" in all States except Hawaii, where they are considered big game.

Participants—Individuals who engage in fishing, hunting, or a wildlife-watching activity. Unless otherwise stated, a person has to have hunted, fished, or wildlife watched in 2011 to be considered a participant.

Plantings—See "Maintain plantings."

Primary purpose—The principal motivation for an activity, trip, or expenditure.

Private land—Land owned by a business, nongovernmental organization, private individual, or a group of individuals such as an association or club.

Public land—Land that is owned by local governments (such as county parks and municipal watersheds),

State governments (such as State parks and wildlife management areas), or the federal government (such as National Forests, Recreational Areas, and Wildlife Refuges).

Residents—Individuals who lived in the State being reported. For example, a person who lives in California and watches whales in California is a residential wildlife watcher in California.

Rural—All territory, population, and housing units located outside of urbanized areas and urban clusters, as determined by the U.S. Census Bureau.

Saltwater—Oceans, tidal bays and sounds, and the tidal portions of rivers and streams.

Screening interviews—The first Survey contact with a sample household. Screening interviews are conducted with a household representative to identify respondents who are eligible for in-depth interviews. Screening interviews gather data such as age and sex about individuals in the households. Further information on screening interviews is available on page vii in the "Survey Background and Method" section of this report.

Small game—Grouse, pheasants, quail, rabbits, squirrels, and similar small animals for which States have small game seasons and bag limits.

Special equipment—Big-ticket equipment items that are owned primarily for wildlife-related recreation:

Bass boats

Other types of motor boats

Canoes and other types of nonmotor boats

Boat motors, boat trailer/hitches, and other boat accessories

Pickups, campers, vans, travel or tent trailers, motor homes, house trailers, recreational vehicles (RVs)

Cabins

Off-the-road vehicles such as trail bikes, all terrain vehicles (ATVs), dune buggies, four-wheelers, 4x4 vehicles, and snowmobiles

Other special equipment

Spenders—Individuals who spent money on fishing, hunting, or wildlife-watching activities or equipment and also participated in those activities.

Sportspersons—Individuals who engaged in fishing, hunting, or both.

Trip—An outing involving fishing, hunting, or wildlife watching. A trip may begin from an individual's principal residence or from another place, such as a vacation home or the home of a relative. A trip may last an hour, a day, or many days.

Type of fishing—There are three types of fishing: (1) freshwater except Great Lakes, (2) Great Lakes, and (3) saltwater.

Type of hunting—There are four types of hunting: (1) big game, (2) small game, (3) migratory bird, and (4) other animal.

Unspecified expenditure—An item that was purchased for use in both fishing and hunting, rather than primarily one or the other. Auxiliary equipment, special equipment, magazines and books, and membership dues and contributions are the items for which a purchase could be categorized as "unspecified."

Urban—All territory, population, and housing units located within boundaries that encompass densely settled territory, consisting of core census block groups or blocks that have a population density of at least 1,000 people per square mile and surrounding census blocks that have an overall density of at least 500 people per square mile. Under certain conditions, less densely settled territory may be included, as determined by the Census Bureau.

Visit parks or natural areas—A visit to places accessible to the public and that are owned or leased by a governmental entity, nongovernmental organization, business, or a private individual or group such as an association or club.

Wildlife—Animals such as birds, fish, insects, mammals, amphibians, and reptiles that are living in natural or wild environments. Wildlife does not include animals living in aquariums, zoos, and other artificial surroundings or domestic animals such as farm animals or pets.

Wildlife observed, photographed, or fed—Examples of species that wildlife watchers observe, photograph, and/or feed are (1) *Wild birds*—songbirds such as cardinals, robins, warblers, jays, buntings, and sparrows; birds of prey such as hawks, owls, eagles, and falcons; waterfowl such as ducks, geese, and swans; other water birds such as shorebirds, herons, pelicans, and cranes; and other birds such as pheasants, turkeys, road runners, and woodpeckers; (2) *Land mammals*—large land mammals such as bears, bison, deer, moose, and elk; small land mammals such as squirrels, foxes, prairie dogs, and rabbits; (3) *Fish* such as salmon, sharks, and groupers; (4) *Marine mammals* such as whales, dolphins, and manatees; and (5) *Other wildlife* such as butterflies, turtles, spiders, and snakes.

Wildlife-related recreation—Recreational fishing, hunting, and wildlife watching.

Wildlife watching—There are six types of wildlife watching: (1) closely observing, (2) photographing, (3) feeding, (4) visiting parks or natural areas, (5) maintaining plantings, and (6) maintaining natural areas. These activities must be the primary purpose of the trip or the around-the-home undertaking.

Wildlife-watching equipment—Items owned primarily for observing, photographing, or feeding wildlife:

Binoculars and spotting scopes

Cameras, video cameras, special lenses, and other photographic equipment

Film and developing

Commercially prepared and packaged wild bird food

Other bulk food used to feed wild birds

Food for other wildlife

Nest boxes, bird houses, feeders, and baths

Day packs, carrying cases, and special clothing

Other items such as field guides and maps

Appendix B

Appendix B.
2010 Participation of 6- to 15-Year-Olds: Data From Screening Interviews

The 2011 National Survey of Fishing, Hunting, and Wildlife-Associated Recreation was carried out in two phases. The first (or screening) phase began in April 2011. The main purpose of this phase was to collect information about all persons 16 years old and older in order to develop a sample of potential sportspersons and wildlife watchers for the second (or detailed) phase. However, information was also collected on the number of persons 6 to 15 years old who participated in wildlife-related recreation activities in 2010.

It is important to emphasize that the information reported from the 2011 screen relates to activity only up to and including 2010. Also, these data are reported by one household respondent speaking for all household members rather than the actual participants. In addition, these data are based on long-term recall (at least a 12-month recall), which has been found in Survey research (see *Investigation of Possible Recall/Reference Period Bias in National Surveys of Fishing, Hunting and Wildlife-Associated Recreation, December 1989, Westat, Inc.*) to add bias to the resulting estimates. In many cases, longer recall periods result in overestimating participation and expenditures for wildlife-related recreation.

Tables B-1 through B-4 report data on 6- to 15-year-old participants in 2010. Detailed expenditures and recreational activity data were not gathered for the 6- to 15-year-old participants.

Because of differences in methodologies of the screening and the detailed phases of the 2011 Survey, the estimates of the two phases are not comparable. Only participants 16 years old and older were eligible for the detailed phase. The screening phase covered activity for 2010 or earlier; the detailed phase has estimates for only 2011. The detailed phase was a series of interviews of the actual participants conducted at 4- and 8-month intervals. The screening phase was a single interview of one household respondent who reported household events with one year or more recall. The shorter recall period of the detailed phase enabled better data accuracy.

Table B-1. Indiana Residents 6 to 15 Years Old Participating in Fishing and Hunting Both Inside and Outside Indiana: 2010

(Population 6 to 15 years old. Numbers in thousands)

Sportspersons	Sportspersons 6 to 15 years old		
	Number	Percent of sportspersons	Percent of population
Total sportspersons...................	424	100	49
Total anglers	424	100	49
Fished only	387	91	44
Fished and hunted			
Total hunters	...	...	...
Hunted only			
Hunted and fished			

Sample size too small (less than 10) to report data reliably

Note: Detail does not add to total because of multiple responses Column showing percent of sportspersons is based on the "Total sportspersons" row Column showing percent of population is based on the state population 6 to 15 years old, including those who did not fish or hunt Data reported on this table are from screening interviews in which one adult household member responded for household members 6 to 15 years old   The screening interview required the respondent to recall 12 months worth of activity Includes state residents who fished or hunted only in other countries

Table B-2. Selected Characteristics of Indiana Resident Anglers and Hunters 6 to 15 Years Old: 2010

(Population 6 to 15 years old. Numbers in thousands)

Characteristic	Population		Sportspersons (fished or hunted)			Anglers			Hunters		
	Number	Percent	Number	Percent who participated	Percent	Number	Percent who participated	Percent	Number	Percent who participated	Percent
Total persons............................	870	100	424	49	100	424	49	100	...	...	...
Population Density of Residence											
Urban	519	60	*230	*44	*54	*230	*44	*54			
Rural	351	40	193	55	46	193	55	46			
Population Size of Residence											
Metropolitan Statistical Area (MSA)	786	90	401	51	95	401	51	95			
1,000,000 or more	407	47	*186	*46	*44	*186	*46	*44			
250,000 to 999,999	*125	*14	*72	*58	*17	*72	*58	*17			
50,000 to 249,999	255	29	*143	*56	*34	*143	*56	*34			
Outside MSA	*84	*10									
Age											
6 to 8 years	288	33	*152	*53	*36	*152	*53	*36			
9 to 11 years	224	26	*99	*44	*23	*99	*44	*23			
12 to 15 years	358	41	*173	*48	*41	*173	*48	*41			
Sex											
Male	419	48	230	55	54	230	55	54			
Female	451	52	*194	*43	*46	*194	*43	*46			
Ethnicity											
Hispanic	*85	*10									
Non-Hispanic	785	90	385	49	91	385	49	91			
Race											
White	768	88	411	54	97	411	54	97			
African American											
All others	*71	*8									
Annual Household Income											
Less than $20,000	*170	*20									
$20,000 to $29,999											
$30,000 to $39,999	*109	*13									
$40,000 to $49,999											
$50,000 to $74,999	*65	*7	*32	*49	*8	*32	*49	*8			
$75,000 to $99,999	*93	*11	*57	*62	*14	*57	*62	*14			
$100,000 or more	*140	*16	*72	*52	*17	*72	*52	*17			
Not reported	*145	*17									

* Estimate based on a sample size of 10–29   Sample size too small (less than 10) to report data reliably

Note: Percent who participated columns show the percent of each row's population who participated in the activity named by the column (the percent of those living in urban areas who wildlife watched, etc) Remaining percent columns show the percent of each column's participants who are described by the row heading (the percent of wildlife watchers who lived in urban areas, etc) Data reported on this table are from screening interviews in which one adult household member responded for household members 6 to 15 years old   The screening interview required the respondent to recall 12 months worth of activity Includes state residents who wildlife watched only in other countries

Table B-3. Indiana Residents 6 to 15 Years Old Participating in Wildlife Watching Both Inside and Outside Indiana: 2010

(Population 6 to 15 years old. Numbers in thousands)

Participants	Number	Percent of participants	Percent of population
Total participants	344	100	40
Away from home	*96	*28	*11
Around the home	332	96	38
Observe wildlife	298	87	34
Photograph wildlife			
Feed wild birds or other wildlife	*178	*52	*20
Maintain plantings or natural areas			

* Estimate based on a sample size of 10–29   Sample size too small (less than 10) to report data reliably

Note: Detail does not add to total because of multiple responses The column showing percent of participation is based on total participants The column showing percent of population is based on the state population 6 to 15 years old, including those who did not participate in wildlife watching Data reported on this table are from screening interviews in which one adult household member responded for all household members 6 to 15 years old The screening interview required the respondent to recall 12 months worth of activity Includes persons who wildlife watched only in other countries

Table B-4. Selected Characteristics of Indiana Resident Wildlife Watchers 6 to 15 Years Old: 2010

(Population 6 to 15 years old. Numbers in thousands)

Characteristic	Population		Total wildlife watchers			Away from Home			Around the home		
	Number	Percent	Number	Percent who participated	Percent	Number	Percent who participated	Percent	Number	Percent who participated	Percent
Total persons	870	100	344	40	100	*96	*11	*100	332	38	100
Population Density of Residence											
Urban	519	60	*202	*39	*59				*198	*38	*59
Rural	351	40	142	41	41	*38	*11	*39	135	38	41
Population Size of Residence											
Metropolitan Statistical Area (MSA)	786	90	297	38	86	*88	*11	*92	285	36	86
1,000,000 or more	407	47	*157	*39	*46				*149	*37	*45
250,000 to 999,999	*125	*14	*61	*49	*18				*61	*49	*19
50,000 to 249,999	255	29	*78	*31	*23				*75	*29	*23
Outside MSA	*84	*10									
Age											
6 to 8 years	288	33	*131	*46	*38				*128	*44	*38
9 to 11 years	224	26	*76	*34	*22				*72	*32	*22
12 to 15 years	358	41	*137	*38	*40				*133	*37	*40
Sex											
Male	419	48	160	38	46	*43	*10	*44	*152	*36	*46
Female	451	52	*185	*41	*54				*180	*40	*54
Ethnicity											
Hispanic	*85	*10									
Non-Hispanic	785	90	307	39	89	*67	*9	*70	295	38	89
Race											
White	768	88	336	44	98	*96	*13	*100	324	42	98
African American											
All others	*71	*8									
Annual Household Income											
Less than $20,000	*170	*20									
$20,000 to $29,999											
$30,000 to $39,999	*109	*13									
$40,000 to $49,999											
$50,000 to $74,999	*65	*7									
$75,000 to $99,999	*93	*11	*45	*48	*13						
$100,000 or more	*140	*16	*86	*62	*25				*86	*62	*26
Not reported	*145	*17	*44	*30	*13						

* Estimate based on a sample size of 10–29   Sample size too small (less than 10) to report data reliably

Note: Percent who participated columns show the percent of each row's population who participated in the activity named by the column (the percent of those living in urban areas who fished, etc) Remaining percent columns show the percent of each column's participants who are described by the row heading (the percent of anglers who lived in urban areas, etc) Data reported on this table are from screening interviews in which one adult household member responded for household members 6 to 15 years old The screening interview required the respondent to recall 12 months worth of activity Includes state residents who fished or hunted only in other countries

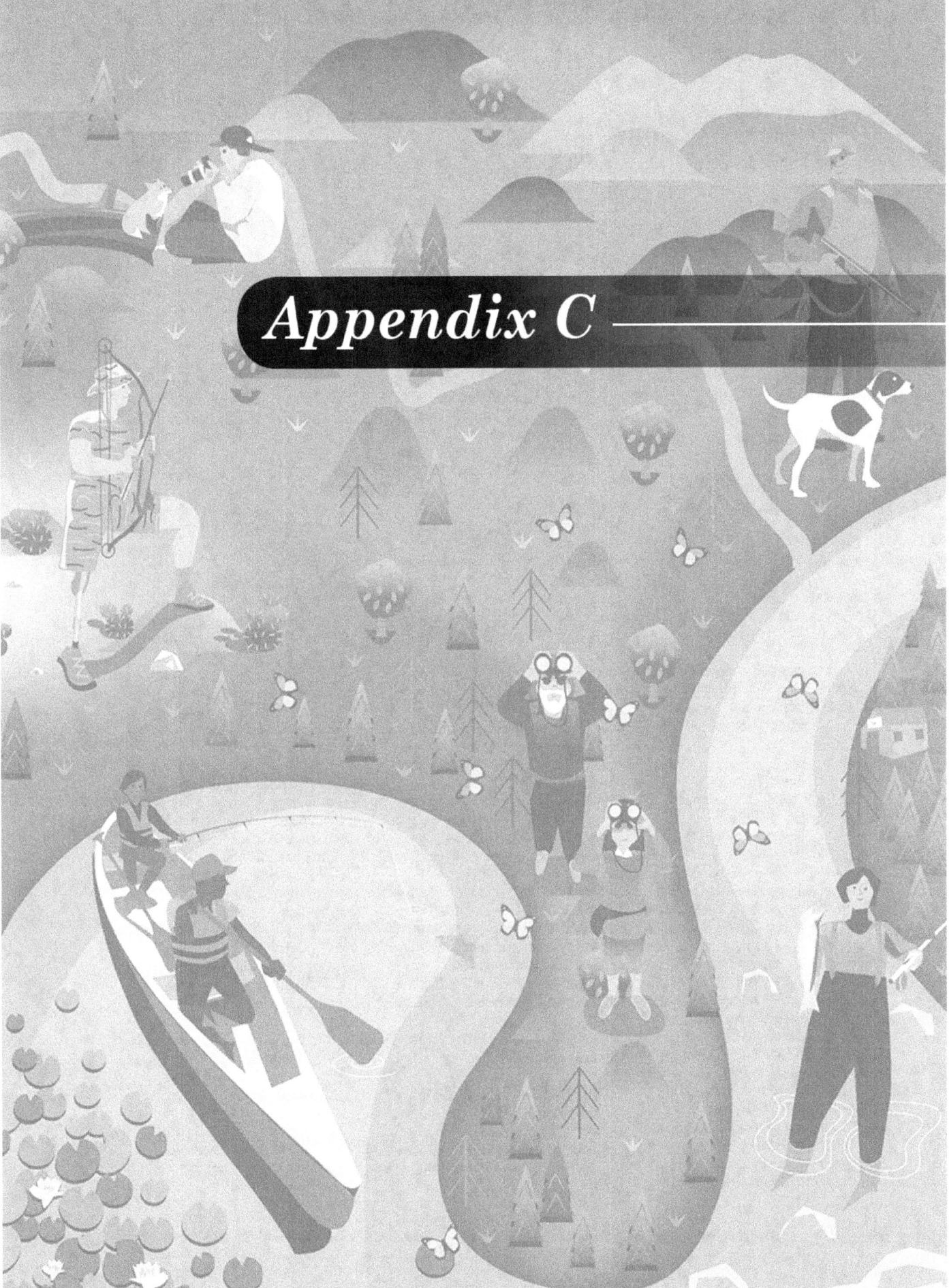

Appendix C

Appendix C.
Significant Methodological Changes From Previous Surveys and Regional Trends

This appendix provides a description of data collection changes and national and regional trend information based on the 1991, 1996, 2001, 2006, and 2011 Surveys. Since these five surveys used similar methodologies, their published information is directly comparable.

Significant Methodological Differences

The most significant design differences in the five Surveys are as follows:

1. The 1991 Survey data was collected by interviewers filling out paper questionnaires. The data entries were keyed in a separate operation after the interview. The 1996, 2001, 2006, and 2011 Survey data were collected by the use of computer-assisted interviews. The questionnaires were programmed into computers, and the interviewer keyed in the responses at the time of the interview.

2. The 1991 Survey screening phase was conducted in January and February of 1991, when a household member of the sample households was interviewed on behalf of the entire household. The screening interviews for the 1996, 2001, and 2006 Surveys were conducted April through June of their survey years in conjunction with the first wave of the detailed interviews. The 2011 Survey also conducted screening interviews and the first detailed interviews April through June of 2011, but furthermore had an additional screening and detailed effort from February 2012 to the end of May 2012. The April–June 2011 screening effort had a high noncontact rate because of poor results using sample telephone numbers obtained from a private firm. Census went back to

the noncontacted component of the original sample in February-May 2012 and interviewed a subsample, requiring annual recall for those respondents. The Wave 3 screen sample was 12,484 of the total 48,600 household screen sample. A modification of the 2011 sampling scheme was to oversample counties that had relatively high proportions of hunting license purchases.

The screening interviews for all five Surveys consisted primarily of demographic questions and wildlife-related recreation questions concerning activity in the previous year (1990, 1995, etc.) and intentions for recreating in the survey year.

In the 1991 Survey, an attempt was made to contact every sample person in all three detailed interview waves. In 1996, 2001, 2006, and 2011 respondents who were interviewed in the first detailed interview wave were not contacted again until the third wave (unless they were part of the other subsample, i.e., a respondent in both the sportsperson and wildlife watching subsamples could be in the first and third wave of sportsperson interviewing and the second and third wave of wildlife watching interviewing). Also, all interviews in the second wave were conducted only by telephone. In-person interviews were only conducted in the first and third waves. The 2011 wave 3 screen phase was composed of both telephone and in-person interviews.

Section I. Important Instrument Changes in the 1996 Survey

1. The 1991 Survey collected information on all wildlife-related recreation purchases made by participants without reference to where the purchase was made. The

1996 Survey asked in which state the purchase was made.

2. In 1991, respondents were asked what kind of fishing they did, i.e., Great Lakes, other freshwater, or saltwater, and then were asked in what states they fished. In 1996, respondents were asked in which states they fished and then were asked what kind of fishing they did. This method had the advantage of not asking about, for example, saltwater fishing when they only fished in a noncoastal state.

3. In 1991, respondents were asked how many days they "actually" hunted or fished for a particular type of game or fish and then how many days they "chiefly" hunted or fished for the same type of game or fish rather than another type of game or fish. To get total days of hunting or fishing for a particular type of game or fish, the "actually" day response was used, while to get the sum of all days of hunting or fishing, the "chiefly" days were summed. In 1996, respondents were asked their total days of hunting or fishing in the country and each state, then how many days they hunted or fished for a particular type of game or fish.

4. Trip-related and equipment expenditure categories were not the same for all Surveys. "Guide fee" and "Pack trip or package fee" were two separate trip-related expenditure items in 1991, while they were combined into one category in the 1996 Survey. "Boating costs" was added to the 1996 hunting and wildlife-watching trip-related expenditure sections. "Heating and cooking fuel" was added to all of the trip-related expenditure sections. "Spearfishing equipment"

was moved from a separate category to the "other" list. "Rods" and "Reels" were two separate categories in 1991 but were combined in 1996. "Lines, hooks, sinkers, etc." was one category in 1991 but split into "Lines" and "Hooks, sinkers, etc." in 1996. "Food used to feed other wildlife" was added to the wildlife-watching equipment section, "Boats" and "Cabins" were added to the wildlife-watching special equipment section, and "Land leasing and ownership" was added to the wildlife-watching expenditures section.

5. Questions asking sportspersons if they participated as much as they wanted were added in 1996. If the sportspersons said no, they were asked why not.

6. The 1991 Survey included questions about participation in organized fishing competitions; anglers using bows and arrows, nets or seines, or spearfishing; hunters using pistols or handguns and target shooting in preparation for hunting. These questions were not asked in 1996.

7. The 1996 Survey included questions about catch and release fishing and persons with disabilities participating in wildlife-related recreation. These questions were not part of the 1991 Survey.

8. The 1991 Survey included questions about average distance traveled to recreation sites. These questions were not included in the 1996 Survey.

9. The 1996 Survey included questions about the last trip the respondent took. Included were questions about the type of trip, where the activity took place, and the distance and direction to the site visited. These questions were not asked in 1991.

10. The 1991 Survey collected data on hunting, fishing, and wildlife watching by U.S. residents in Canada. The 1996 Survey collected data on fishing and wildlife-watching by U.S. residents in Canada.

Section II. Important Instrument Changes in the 2001 Survey

1. The 1991 and 1996 single race category "Asian or Pacific Islander" was changed to two categories "Asian" and "Native Hawaiian or Other Pacific Islander." In 1991 and 1996, the respondent was required to pick only one category, while in 2001 the respondent could pick any combination of categories. The next question stipulated that the respondent could only be identified with one category and then asked what that category was.

2. The 1991 and 1996 land leasing and ownership sections asked the respondent to combine the two types of land use into one and give total acreage and expenditures. In 2001, the two types of land use were explored separately.

3. The 1991 and 1996 wildlife-watching sections included questions on birdwatching for around-the-home participants only. The 2001 Survey added a question on birdwatching for away-from-home participants. Also, questions on the use of birding life lists and how many species the respondent can identify were added.

4. "Recreational vehicles" was added to the sportspersons and wildlife-watchers special equipment section. "House trailer" was added to the sportspersons special equipment section.

5. Total personal income was asked in the detailed phase of the 1996 Survey. This was changed to total household income in the 2001 Survey.

6. A question was added to the trip-related expenditures section to ascertain how much of the total was spent in the respondent's state of residence when the respondent participated in hunting, fishing, or wildlife watching out-of-state.

7. Boating questions were added to the fishing section. The respondent was asked about the extent of boat usage for the three types of fishing.

8. The 1996 Survey included questions about the months around-the-home wildlife watchers fed birds. These questions were not repeated in the 2001 Survey.

9. The contingent valuation sections of the three types of wildlife-related recreation were altered, using an open-ended question format instead of 1996's dichotomous choice format.

Section III. Important Instrument Changes in the 2006 Survey

1. A series of boating questions was added. The new questions dealt with anglers using motorboats and/or nonmotorboats, length of boat used most often, distance to boat launch used most often, needed improvements to facilities at the launch, whether or not the respondent completed a boating safety course, who the boater fished with most often, and the source and type of information the boater used for his or her fishing.

2. Questions regarding catch and release fishing were added. They were whether or not the respondent caught and released fish and, if so, the percent of fish released.

3. The proportion of hunting done with a rifle or shotgun, as contrasted with muzzleloader or archery equipment, was asked.

4. In the contingent valuation section, where the value of wildlife-related recreation was determined, two quality-variable questions were added: the average length of certain fish caught and whether a deer, elk, or moose was killed. Plus the economic evaluation bid questions were rephrased, from "What is the most your [species] hunting in [State name] could have cost you per trip last year before you would NOT have gone [species] hunting at all in 2001, not even one trip, because it would have been too expensive?", for the hunters, for example, to "What is the cost that would have prevented you from taking even one such trip in 2006? In other words, if the trip cost was below this amount, you would have gone [species] hunting in [State name], but if the trip cost was above this amount, you would not have gone."

5. Questions concerning hunting, fishing, or wildlife watching in other countries were taken out of the Survey.

6. Questions about the reasons for not going hunting or fishing, or not going as much as expected, were deleted.

7. Disability of participants questions were taken out.

8. Determination of the types of sites for wildlife watching was discontinued.

9. The birding questions regarding the use of birding life lists and the ability to identify birds based on their sight or sounds were deleted.

10. Public transportation costs were divided into two sections, "public transportation by airplane" and "other public transportation, including trains, buses, and car rentals, etc.".

Section IV. Important Instrument Changes in the 2011 Survey

1. The series of boating questions added in 2006 was deleted.

2. Questions about target shooting and the usage of a shooting range in preparation for hunting were added. The types of weapon used at the shooting range were quantified.

3. Questions about plantings expenditures for the purpose of hunting were added.

4. "Feral pig" was recategorized from big game to other animals for all states except Hawaii.

5. "Ptarmigan" was included as its own small game category, instead of lumped in "other."

6. In previous Surveys, "Moose" was included as its own category only for Alaska. For 2011, "Moose" was included as its own big game category, instead of lumped in "other," for all fifty states.

7. In previous Surveys, "Wolf" was included as its own category only for Alaska. For 2011, "Wolf" was included as its own other animal category, instead of lumped in "other," for all fifty states.

8. The household income categories were modified. The top categories were changed from "$100,000 or more" to "$100,000 to $149,999" and "$150,000 or more."

9. The "Steelhead" category was deleted from the saltwater fish species section, with the idea that it would be included in "other."

10. The 2006 around-the-home wildlife-watching category that quantified visitors of "public parks or areas" was rewritten to wildlife watching at "parks or natural areas." This change was to make clear that respondents should include recreating at quasi-governmental and private areas.

11. The 2006 wildlife watching equipment category "Film and developing" was rewritten to "Film and photo processing."

Regional Trends

This trends section covers the period from 1991 to 2011. The 1991, 1996, 2001, 2006, and 2011 Surveys used similar methodologies, making all published information for the five Surveys directly comparable.

Table C-1a. Comparison of Wildlife-Related Recreation in the United States: 1991–1996

(U.S. population 16 years old and older. Numbers in thousands. All expenditures in 2011 dollars. 1996 expenditures categories made comparable to 1991)

Participants, days, and expenditures	1991 (number)	1996 (number)	1991–1996 percent change
Hunting			
Hunters, total	14,063	13,975	NS–1
Hunting days, total	235,806	256,676	NS9
Hunting expenditures, total	$20,399,152	$29,259,999	43
Fishing			
Anglers, total	35,578	35,246	NS–1
Fishing days, total	511,329	625,893	22
Fishing expenditures, total	$39,669,337	$54,224,581	37
Wildlife Watching			
Wildlife watchers, total	76,111	62,868	–17
Around the home	73,904	60,751	–18
Away from home	29,999	23,652	–21
Wildlife-watching days, away from home	342,406	313,790	NS–8
Wildlife-watching expenditures, total	$30,574,499	$36,924,875	21

NS Not different from zero at the 5 percent level of significance

Table C-1b. Comparison of Wildlife-Related Recreation in the United States: 1996–2001

(U.S. population 16 years old and older. Numbers in thousands. All expenditures in 2011 dollars. 1996 and 2001 expenditures categories made comparable to 1991)

Participants, days, and expenditures	1996 (number)	2001 (number)	1996–2001 percent change
Hunting			
Hunters, total	13,975	13,034	–7
Hunting days, total	256,676	228,368	–11
Hunting expenditures, total	$29,259,999	$25,993,960	NS–11
Fishing			
Anglers, total	35,246	34,071	–3
Fishing days, total	625,893	557,394	–11
Fishing expenditures, total	$54,224,581	$45,076,739	–17
Wildlife Watching			
Wildlife watchers, total	62,868	66,105	5
Around the home	60,751	62,928	4
Away from home	23,652	21,823	–8
Wildlife-watching days, away from home	313,790	372,006	19
Wildlife-watching expenditures, total	$36,924,875	$42,904,872	16

NS Not different from zero at the 5 percent level of significance

Table C-1c. Comparison of Wildlife-Related Recreation in the United States: 2001–2006

(U.S. population 16 years old and older. Numbers in thousands. All expenditures in 2011 dollars. 2001 and 2006 expenditures categories made comparable to 1991)

Participants, days, and expenditures	2001 (number)	2006 (number)	2001–2006 percent change
Hunting			
Hunters, total	13,034	12,510	NS-4
Hunting days, total	228,368	219,925	NS-4
Hunting expenditures, total	$25,993,960	$25,265,523	NS-3
Fishing			
Anglers, total	34,071	29,952	-12
Fishing days, total	557,394	516,781	-7
Fishing expenditures, total	$45,076,739	$46,909,364	NS4
Wildlife Watching			
Wildlife watchers, total	66,105	71,132	8
Around the home	62,928	67,756	8
Away from home	21,823	22,977	NS5
Wildlife-watching days, away from home	372,006	352,070	NS-5
Wildlife-watching expenditures, total	$42,904,872	$40,023,078	NS-7

NS Not different from zero at the 5 percent level of significance

Table C-1d. Comparison of Wildlife-Related Recreation in the United States: 2006–2011

(U.S. population 16 years old and older. Numbers in thousands. All expenditures in 2011 dollars. 2006 and 2011 expenditures categories made comparable to 1991)

Participants, days, and expenditures	2006 (number)	2011 (number)	2006–2011 percent change
Hunting			
Hunters, total	12,510	13,674	9
Hunting days, total	219,925	281,884	28
Hunting expenditures, total	$25,265,523	$32,579,640	29
Fishing			
Anglers, total	29,952	33,112	11
Fishing days, total	516,781	553,841	NS7
Fishing expenditures, total	$46,909,364	$41,624,599	NS-11
Wildlife Watching			
Wildlife watchers, total	71,132	71,776	NS1
Around the home	67,756	68,598	NS1
Away from home	22,977	22,496	NS-2
Wildlife-watching days, away from home	352,070	335,625	NS-5
Wildlife-watching expenditures, total	$40,023,078	$43,636,608	NS9

NS Not different from zero at the 5 percent level of significance

Table C-1e. Comparison of Wildlife-Related Recreation in the United States: 1991–2011

(U.S. population 16 years old and older. Numbers in thousands. All expenditures in 2011 dollars. 2011 expenditures categories made comparable to 1991)

Participants, days, and expenditures	1991 (number)	2011 (number)	1991–2011 percent change
Hunting			
Hunters, total	14,063	13,674	[NS]3
Hunting days, total	235,806	281,884	20
Hunting expenditures, total	$20,399,152	$32,579,640	60
Fishing			
Anglers, total	35,578	33,112	–7
Fishing days, total	511,329	553,841	8
Fishing expenditures, total	$39,669,337	$41,624,599	[NS]5
Wildlife Watching			
Wildlife watchers, total	76,111	71,776	–6
Around the home	73,904	68,598	–7
Away from home	29,999	22,496	–25
Wildlife-watching days, away from home	342,406	335,625	[NS]–2
Wildlife-watching expenditures, total	$30,574,499	$43,636,608	43

[NS] Not different from zero at the 5 percent level of significance

Table C-2. Anglers and Hunters by Census Division: 1991, 1996, 2001, 2006, and 2011

(U.S. population 16 years old and older. Numbers in thousands)

Area and sportsperson	1991 Number	1991 Percent	1996 Number	1996 Percent	2001 Number	2001 Percent	2006 Number	2006 Percent	2011 Number	2011 Percent
UNITED STATES										
Total population	189,964	100	201,472	100	212,298	100	229,245	100	239,313	100
Sportspersons	39,979	21	39,694	20	37,805	18	33,916	15	37,397	16
Anglers	35,578	19	35,246	17	34,067	16	29,952	13	33,112	14
Hunters	14,063	7	13,975	7	13,034	6	12,510	5	13,674	6
New England										
Total population	10,180	100	10,306	100	10,575	100	11,233	100	11,593	100
Sportspersons	1,658	16	1,673	16	1,504	14	1,353	12	1,441	12
Anglers	1,545	15	1,520	15	1,402	13	1,246	11	1,355	12
Hunters	444	4	465	5	386	4	374	3	420	4
Middle Atlantic										
Total population	29,216	100	29,371	100	29,806	100	31,518	100	32,392	100
Sportspersons	4,508	15	4,192	14	3,810	13	3,214	10	3,966	12
Anglers	3,871	13	3,627	12	3,250	11	2,550	8	3,496	11
Hunters	1,746	6	1,453	5	1,633	5	1,520	5	1,558	5
East North Central										
Total population	32,188	100	33,121	100	34,082	100	35,609	100	36,199	100
Sportspersons	7,202	22	6,912	21	6,400	19	5,975	17	6,766	19
Anglers	6,264	19	6,006	18	5,655	17	5,190	15	5,861	16
Hunters	2,789	9	2,712	8	2,421	7	2,376	7	2,688	7
West North Central										
Total population	13,504	100	13,875	100	14,430	100	15,458	100	15,860	100
Sportspersons	4,143	31	3,977	29	4,239	29	3,836	25	3,980	25
Anglers	3,647	27	3,416	25	3,836	27	3,284	21	3,591	23
Hunters	1,709	13	1,917	14	1,710	12	1,779	12	1,661	10
South Atlantic										
Total population	33,682	100	36,776	100	39,286	100	43,965	100	46,417	100
Sportspersons	6,996	21	7,282	20	6,957	18	6,633	15	6,749	15
Anglers	6,441	19	6,636	18	6,451	16	6,116	14	6,163	13
Hunters	2,083	6	2,050	6	1,875	5	1,884	4	1,870	4
East South Central										
Total population	11,667	100	12,459	100	12,976	100	13,722	100	14,206	100
Sportspersons	2,984	26	2,907	23	2,865	22	2,689	20	3,010	21
Anglers	2,635	23	2,514	20	2,543	20	2,436	18	2,444	17
Hunters	1,279	11	1,301	10	1,164	9	1,101	8	1,531	11
West South Central										
Total population	19,926	100	21,811	100	23,337	100	25,407	100	27,195	100
Sportspersons	5,125	26	5,093	23	4,924	21	4,499	18	4,855	18
Anglers	4,592	23	4,616	21	4,375	19	3,952	16	4,298	16
Hunters	1,843	9	1,812	8	1,988	9	1,810	7	1,909	7
Mountain										
Total population	10,092	100	11,966	100	13,308	100	15,651	100	17,013	100
Sportspersons	2,488	25	2,761	23	2,757	21	2,372	15	2,976	17
Anglers	2,079	21	2,411	20	2,443	18	2,084	13	2,586	15
Hunters	1,069	11	1,061	9	1,020	8	868	6	1,043	6
Pacific										
Total population	29,508	100	31,787	100	34,498	100	36,681	100	38,438	100
Sportspersons	4,875	17	4,897	15	4,349	13	3,345	9	3,654	10
Anglers	4,505	15	4,501	14	4,111	12	3,094	8	3,319	9
Hunters	1,101	4	1,203	4	837	2	798	2	996	3

Table C-3. Wildlife-Watching Participants by Census Division: 1991, 1996, 2001, 2006, and 2011

(U.S. population 16 years old and older. Numbers in thousands)

Area and wildlife watcher	1991 Number	1991 Percent	1996 Number	1996 Percent	2001 Number	2001 Percent	2006 Number	2006 Percent	2011 Number	2011 Percent
UNITED STATES										
Total population	189,964	100	201,472	100	212,298	100	229,245	100	239,313	100
Total wildlife watchers	76,111	40	62,868	31	66,105	31	71,132	31	71,776	30
Away from home	29,999	16	23,652	12	21,823	10	22,977	10	22,496	9
Around the home	73,904	39	60,751	30	62,928	30	67,756	30	68,598	29
New England										
Total population	10,180	100	10,306	100	10,575	100	11,233	100	11,593	100
Total wildlife watchers	4,598	45	3,710	36	3,875	37	4,489	40	3,954	34
Away from home	1,856	18	1,443	14	1,155	11	1,340	12	1,187	10
Around the home	4,544	45	3,586	35	3,765	36	4,310	38	3,858	33
Middle Atlantic										
Total population	29,216	100	29,371	100	29,806	100	31,518	100	32,392	100
Total wildlife watchers	10,556	36	8,185	28	8,740	29	8,723	28	9,118	28
Away from home	4,166	14	2,960	10	2,849	10	2,729	9	2,561	8
Around the home	10,282	35	8,023	27	8,452	28	8,451	27	8,744	27
East North Central										
Total population	32,188	100	33,121	100	34,082	100	35,609	100	36,199	100
Total wildlife watchers	14,511	45	11,731	35	11,631	34	12,215	34	12,840	35
Away from home	5,572	17	4,501	14	3,571	10	3,792	11	3,168	9
Around the home	14,175	44	11,297	34	11,196	33	11,845	33	12,492	35
West North Central										
Total population	13,504	100	13,875	100	14,430	100	15,458	100	15,860	100
Total wildlife watchers	6,924	51	5,089	37	6,206	43	6,741	44	5,479	35
Away from home	2,654	20	1,927	14	2,059	14	2,163	14	1,783	11
Around the home	6,722	50	4,900	35	5,938	41	6,447	42	5,201	33
South Atlantic										
Total population	33,682	100	36,776	100	39,286	100	43,965	100	46,417	100
Total wildlife watchers	13,047	39	11,252	31	11,395	29	12,862	29	13,315	29
Away from home	4,450	13	3,992	11	3,469	9	3,208	7	4,393	9
Around the home	12,813	38	10,964	30	10,911	28	12,432	28	12,767	28
East South Central										
Total population	11,667	100	12,459	100	12,976	100	13,722	100	14,206	100
Total wildlife watchers	4,864	42	3,904	31	4,514	35	4,931	36	4,663	33
Away from home	1,592	14	1,118	9	1,086	8	1,758	13	1,456	10
Around the home	4,765	41	3,795	30	4,390	34	4,683	34	4,394	31
West South Central										
Total population	19,926	100	21,811	100	23,337	100	25,407	100	27,195	100
Total wildlife watchers	7,035	35	5,933	27	5,747	25	6,764	27	7,164	26
Away from home	2,459	12	2,096	10	1,822	8	2,127	8	1,728	6
Around the home	6,817	34	5,773	26	5,490	24	6,319	25	7,087	26
Mountain										
Total population	10,092	100	11,966	100	13,308	100	15,651	100	17,013	100
Total wildlife watchers	4,437	44	4,099	34	4,619	35	4,968	32	5,189	30
Away from home	2,215	22	1,967	16	2,019	15	2,004	13	2,230	13
Around the home	4,145	41	3,855	32	4,282	32	4,605	29	4,716	28
Pacific										
Total population	29,508	100	31,787	100	34,498	100	36,681	100	38,438	100
Total wildlife watchers	10,139	34	8,966	28	9,377	27	9,439	26	10,054	26
Away from home	5,035	17	3,648	11	3,793	11	3,856	11	3,990	10
Around the home	9,641	33	8,558	27	8,504	25	8,664	24	9,337	24

Appendix D

Appendix D.
Sample Design and Statistical Accuracy

This appendix is presented in two parts. The first part is the U.S. Census Bureau Source and Accuracy Statement. This statement describes the sampling design for the 2011 Survey and highlights the steps taken to produce estimates from the completed questionnaires. The statement explains the use of standard errors and confidence intervals. It also provides comprehensive information about errors characteristic of surveys and formulas and parameters to calculate an approximate standard error or confidence interval for each number published in this report. The second part, Tables D-1 and D-2, reports estimates and approximate standard errors for selected measures of participation and expenditures for wildlife-related recreation.

Source and Accuracy Statement for the Indiana State Report of the *2011 National Survey of Fishing, Hunting, and Wildlife-Associated Recreation*

SOURCE OF DATA

The estimates in this report are based on data collected in the *2011 National Survey of Fishing, Hunting, and Wildlife-Associated Recreation* (FHWAR) conducted by the Census Bureau and sponsored by the U.S. Fish and Wildlife Service.

The eligible universe for the FHWAR is the civilian noninstitutionalized and nonbarrack military population living in the United States. The institutionalized population, which is excluded from the population universe, is composed primarily of the population in correctional institutions and nursing homes (98 percent of the 4 million institutionalized people in Census 2010).

The 2011 FHWAR was designed to provide state-level estimates of the number of participants in recreational

hunting and fishing and in wildlife watching activities (e.g., wildlife observation). Information was collected on the number of participants, where and how often they participated, the type of wildlife encountered, and the amounts of money spent on wildlife-related recreation.

The survey was conducted in two stages: an initial screening of households to identify likely sportspersons and wildlife-watching participants and a series of follow-up interviews of selected persons to collect detailed data about their wildlife-related recreation during 2011.

SAMPLE DESIGN

The 2011 FHWAR sample was selected from the Census Bureau's master address file (MAF).

The FHWAR is a multistage probability sample, with coverage in all 50 states and the District of Columbia.[1] In the first stage of the sampling process, primary sampling units (PSUs) are selected for sample. The PSUs are defined to correspond to the Office of Management and Budget definitions of Core Based Statistical Area definitions and to improve efficiency in field operations. The United States is divided into 2,025 PSUs. These PSUs are grouped into 824 strata. Within each stratum, a single PSU is chosen for the sample, with its probability of selection proportional to its population as of the 2000 decennial census. This PSU represents the entire stratum from which it was selected. In the case of strata consisting of only one PSU, the PSU is chosen with certainty.

Within the selected PSUs, the FHWAR sample was selected from the MAF.

FHWAR Screening Sample

The total screening sample in Indiana consisted of **802** households. Interviewing for the screen was conducted during April, May, and June 2011. Due to a high noncontact rate, an additional personal visit screening interview, for a subsample of noncontact cases, occurred again in February, March, April, or May 2012. Of all housing units in sample, about **709** were determined to be eligible for interview. Interviewers obtained interviews at **548** of these units for an Indiana response rate of **77** percent.[2] Indiana's weighted response rate was **84** percent. The interviewers asked screening questions for all household members 6 years old and older. Noninterviews occur when the occupants are not found at home after repeated calls or are unavailable for some other reason.

Data for the FHWAR sportspersons sample and wildlife-watchers sample were collected in three waves.[3] The first wave started in April 2011, the second in September 2011, and the third in January 2012. In the sportspersons sample, all persons who hunted or fished in 2011 by the time of the screening interview were interviewed in the first wave. The remaining sportspersons in sample were interviewed in the second wave. The reference period was the preceding 4 months for waves 1 and 2. In wave 3, the reference period was either 4, 8, or 12 months depending on when the sample person was first interviewed.

---

[1] The sample size in the District of Columbia (D C) is not of sufficient size to produce reliable estimates for only D C The sample responses from D C are included in the U S totals for complete coverage of the U S (excluding Puerto Rico and the U S Virgin Islands)

[2] Response rates are calculated by using APPOR's RR2 formula

[3] The sample cases selected due to high noncontact rates were only interviewed once They received a screener and if they had some form of participation a detailed questionnaire These participants did not get three waves of interviewing The reference period for these sampled cases was between 13 and 16 months

Detailed Samples

Two independent detailed samples were chosen from the FHWAR screening sample. One consisted of sportspersons (people who hunt or fish) and the other of wildlife watchers (people who observe, photograph, or feed wildlife).

A. Sportspersons

The Census Bureau selected the detailed samples based on information reported during the screening phase. Based on information collected from the household respondent, every person 16 years old and older in the FHWAR screening sample was assigned to a sportspersons stratum. The criteria for the strata included time devoted to hunting or fishing in previous years, participation in hunting or fishing in 2011 by the time of the screening interview, and intentions to participate in hunting and fishing activities during the remainder of 2011.[4] The four sportspersons categories were:

1. *Active*—a person who had already participated in hunting or fishing in 2011 at the time of the screener interview.

2. *Likely*—a person who had not participated in 2011 at the time of the screener, but had participated in 2010 OR was likely to participate in 2011.

3. *Inactive*—a person who had not participated in 2010 or 2011 AND was somewhat unlikely to participate in 2011.

4. *Nonparticipant*—a person who had not participated in 2010 or 2011 AND was very unlikely to participate in 2011.

Due to the high noncontact rates in wave 1, all persons in the active, likely, and inactive groups were selected with certainty.

Active sportspersons were given the detailed interview twice—at the time of the screening interview (in April, May, or June 2011) and again in January or February 2012.[5] Likely sportspersons and inactive sportspersons were also interviewed

twice—first in September or October 2011, then in January or February 2012. Persons in the nonparticipant group were not eligible for a detailed interview. About **313** persons were designated for interviews in Indiana. The detailed sportspersons sample sizes varied by state to get reliable state-level estimates. During each interview period, about **31** percent of the designated persons were not found at home or were unavailable for some other reason. Overall, about **216** detailed sportspersons interviews were completed at a response rate of **69** percent.

B. Wildlife Watchers

The wildlife-watching detailed sample was also selected based on information reported during the screening phase. Based on information collected from the household respondent, every person 16 years old and older was assigned to a stratum. The criteria for the strata included time devoted to wildlife watching activities in previous years, participation in wildlife watching activities in 2011 by the time of the screening interview, and intentions to participate in wildlife watching activities during the remainder of 2011.[6] The five wildlife-watching categories were:

1. *Active*—a person who had already participated in 2011 at the time of the screening interview.

2. *Avid*—a person who had not yet participated in 2011, but in 2010 had taken trips to participate in wildlife-watching activities for 21 or more days or had spent $300 or more.

3. *Average*—a person who had not yet participated in 2011, but in 2010 had taken trips to wildlife watch for less than 21 days and had spent less than $300 OR had not participated in wildlife-watching activities but was very likely to in the remainder of 2011.

4. *Infrequent*—a person who had not participated in 2010 or 2011, but was somewhat

likely or somewhat unlikely to participate in the remainder of 2011.

5. *Nonparticipant*—a person who had not participated in 2010 or 2011 AND was very unlikely to participate during the remainder of 2011.

Persons were selected for the detailed sample based on these groupings, but persons in the nonparticipant group were not eligible for a detailed interview.

A subsample of each of the other groups was selected to receive a detailed interview with the chance of selection diminishing as the likelihood of participation diminished. Wildlife-watching participants were given the detailed interview twice.[7] Some received their first detailed interview at the same time as the screening interview (in April, May, or June 2011). The rest received their first detailed interview in September or October 2011. All wildlife-watching participants received their second interview in January or February 2012. Some respondents were given the screener and detailed interview in February, March, April, or May 2012. About **244** persons were designated for interviews in Indiana. The detailed wildlife-watching sample sizes varied by state to get reliable state-level estimates. During each interview period, about **31** percent of the designated persons were not found at home or were unavailable for some other reason. Overall, about **168** detailed wildlife watcher interviews were completed at a response rate of **69** percent.

ESTIMATION PROCEDURE

Several stages of adjustments were used to derive the final 2011 FHWAR person weights. A brief description of the major components of the weights is given below. All statistics for the population 6 to 15 years of age were derived from the screening interview. Statistics for the population 16 years old and older come from both the screening and detailed interviews. Estimates that come from the screening sample are presented in Appendix B.

---

[4] The sample cases selected due to high noncontact rates were not assigned a sportsperson stratum

[5] The sample cases selected due to high noncontact rates were given the detailed sportsperson interview once

[6] The sample cases selected due to high noncontact rates were not assigned a wildlife watcher stratum Wildlife-watching participants in these cases were then subsampled into the detailed questionnaire

[7] The sample cases selected due to high noncontact rates were given the detailed wildlife-watching interview once

A. Screening Sample

Every interviewed person in the screening sample received a screening weight that was the product of the following factors:

1. *Base Weight.* The base weight is the inverse of the household's probability of selection.

2. *Household Noninterview Adjustment.* The noninterview adjustment inflates the weight assigned to interviewed households to account for households eligible for interview but for which no interview was obtained.

3. *First-Stage Adjustment.* The 824 areas designated for our samples were selected from 2,025 such areas of the United States. Some sample areas represent only themselves and are referred to as self-representing. The remaining areas represent other areas similar in selected characteristics and are thus designated non-self-representing. The first-stage factor reduces the component of variation arising from sampling the non-self-representing areas.

4. *Second-Stage Adjustment.* This adjustment brings the estimates of the total population into agreement with census-based estimates of the civilian noninstitutionalized and nonbarrack military populations for each state.

B. Sportspersons Sample

Every interviewed person in the sportspersons detailed sample received a weight that was the product of the following factors:

1. *Screening Weight.* This is the person's final weight from the screening sample.

2. *Sportspersons Stratum Adjustment.* This factor inflates the weights of persons selected for the detailed sample to account for the subsampling done within each sportsperson stratum.

3. *Sportspersons Noninterview Adjustment.* This factor adjusts

the weights of the interviewed sportspersons to account for sportspersons selected for the detailed sample for whom no interview was obtained. A person was considered a noninterview if he or she was not interviewed in the third wave of interviewing.

4. *Sportspersons Ratio Adjustment Factor.* This is a ratio adjustment of the detailed sample to the screening sample within the sportspersons sampling strata. This adjustment brings the population estimates of persons aged 16 years old and older from the detailed sample into agreement with the same estimates from the screening sample, which was a much larger sample.

C. Wildlife-Watchers Sample

Every interviewed person in the wildlife-watchers detailed sample received a weight that was the product of the following factors:

1. *Screening Weight.* This is the person's final weight from the screening sample.

2. *Wildlife-Watchers Stratum Adjustment.* This factor inflates the weights of persons selected for the detailed sample to account for the subsampling done within each wildlife watcher stratum.

3. *Wildlife-Watchers Noninterview Adjustment.* This factor adjusts the weights of the interviewed wildlife-watching participants to account for wildlife watchers selected for the detailed sample for whom no interview was obtained. A person was considered a noninterview if he or she was not interviewed in the third wave of interviewing.

4. *Wildlife-Watchers Ratio Adjustment Factor.* This is a ratio adjustment of the detailed sample to the screening sample within the wildlife-watchers sampling strata. This adjustment brings the population estimates of persons aged 16 years old and older from the detailed sample into agreement

with the same estimates from the screening sample, which was a much larger sample.

ACCURACY OF THE ESTIMATES

A sample survey estimate has two types of error: sampling and nonsampling. The accuracy of an estimate depends on both types of error. The nature of the sampling error is known given the survey design; the full extent of the nonsampling error is unknown.

NONSAMPLING ERROR

For a given estimator, the difference between the estimate that would result if the sample were to include the entire population and the true population value being estimated is known as nonsampling error. There are several sources of nonsampling error that may occur during the development or execution of the survey. It can occur because of circumstances created by the interviewer, the respondent, the survey instrument, or the way the data are collected and processed. For example, errors could occur because:

- The interviewer records the wrong answer, the respondent provides incorrect information, the respondent estimates the requested information, or an unclear survey question is misunderstood by the respondent (measurement error).

- Some individuals who should have been included in the survey frame were missed (coverage error).

- Responses are not collected from all those in the sample or the respondent is unwilling to provide information (nonresponse error).

- Values are estimated imprecisely for missing data (imputation error).

- Forms may be lost; data may be incorrectly keyed, coded, or recoded, etc. (processing error).

The Census Bureau employs quality control procedures throughout the production process, including the overall design of surveys, the wording of questions, the review of the work of interviewers and coders, and the statistical review of reports to minimize these errors. Two types of nonsampling

error that can be examined to a limited extent are nonresponse and undercoverage.

Nonresponse. The effect of nonresponse cannot be measured directly, but one indication of its potential effect is the nonresponse rate. For the FHWAR screener interview in Indiana, the household-level nonresponse rate was **23** percent. The person-level nonresponse rate for the detailed sportsperson interview in Indiana was an additional **31** percent and for the wildlife watchers it was **31** percent. Since the screener nonresponse rate is a household-level rate and the detailed interview nonresponse rate is a person-level rate, we cannot combine these rates to derive an overall nonresponse rate. Since the screener nonresponse rate is a household-level rate and the detailed interview nonresponse rate is a person-level rate, we cannot combine these rates to derive an overall nonresponse rate. Since it is unlikely the nonresponding households to the FHWAR have the same number of persons as the households successfully interviewed, combining these rates would result in an overestimate of the "true" person-level overall nonresponse rate for the detailed interviews.

Coverage. Overall screener undercoverage is estimated to be about 13 percent. Ratio estimation to independent population controls, as described previously, partially corrects for the bias due to survey undercoverage. However, biases exist in the estimates to the extent that missed persons in missed households or missed persons in interviewed households have different characteristics from those of interviewed persons in the same age group.

Comparability of Data. Data obtained from the 2011 FHWAR and other sources are not entirely comparable. This results from differences in interviewer training and experience and in differing survey processes. This is an example of nonsampling variability not reflected in the standard errors. Therefore, caution should be used when comparing results from different sources. (See Appendix C.)

A Nonsampling Error Warning. Since the full extent of the nonsampling error is unknown, one should be particularly careful when interpreting results based on small differences between estimates.

The Census Bureau recommends that data users incorporate information about nonsampling errors into their analyses, as nonsampling error could impact the conclusions drawn from the results. Caution should also be used when interpreting results based on a relatively small number of cases. Summary measures (such as medians and percentage distributions) probably do not reveal useful information when computed on a subpopulation smaller than 90,000 for screener data, 100,000 for the detailed sportsperson data, and 235,000 for the wildlife-watchers data.

SAMPLING ERROR

Since the FHWAR estimates come from a sample, they may differ from figures from an enumeration of the entire population using the same questionnaires, instructions, and enumerators. For a given estimator, the difference between an estimate based on a sample and the estimate that would result if the sample were to include the entire population is known as sampling error. Standard errors, as calculated by methods described in "Standard Errors and Their Use," are primarily measures of the magnitude of sampling error. However, they may include some nonsampling error.

Standard Errors and Their Use. The sample estimate and its standard error enable one to construct a confidence interval. A confidence interval is a range that has a known probability of including the average result of all possible samples. For example, if all possible samples were surveyed under essentially the same general conditions and using the same sample design, and if an estimate and its standard error were calculated from each sample, then approximately 95 percent of the intervals from 1.96 standard errors below the estimate to 1.96 standard errors above the estimate would include the average result of all possible samples. A particular confidence interval may or may not contain the average estimate derived from all possible samples. However, one can say with specified confidence that the interval includes the average estimate calculated from all possible samples. Standard errors may also be used to perform hypothesis testing, a procedure for distinguishing between population parameters using sample estimates. The most common type of hypothesis is that the population

parameters are different. An example would be comparing the proportion of anglers to the proportion of hunters. Tests may be performed at various levels of significance. A significance level is the probability of concluding that the characteristics are different when, in fact, they are the same. For example, to conclude that two characteristics are different at the 0.05 level of significance, the absolute value of the estimated difference between characteristics must be greater than or equal to 1.96 times the standard error of the difference. This report uses 95-percent confidence intervals and 0.05 level of significance to determine statistical validity. Consult standard statistical textbooks for alternative criteria.

Estimating Standard Errors. The Census Bureau uses replication methods to estimate the standard errors of FHWAR estimates. These methods primarily measure the magnitude of sampling error. However, they do measure some effects of nonsampling error as well. They do not measure systematic biases in the data associated with nonsampling error. Bias is the average over all possible samples of the differences between the sample estimates and the true value.

Generalized Variance Parameters. While it is possible to compute and present an estimate of the standard error based on the survey data for each estimate in a report, there are a number of reasons why this is not done. A presentation of the individual standard errors would be of limited use, since one could not possibly predict all of the combinations of results that may be of interest to data users. Additionally, data users have access to FHWAR microdata files, and it is impossible to compute in advance the standard error for every estimate one might obtain from those data sets. Moreover, variance estimates are based on sample data and have variances of their own. Therefore, some methods of stabilizing these estimates of variance, for example, by generalizing or averaging over time, may be used to improve their reliability. Experience has shown that certain groups of estimates have similar relationships between their variances and expected values. Modeling or generalizing may provide more stable variance estimates by taking advantage of these similarities. The generalized variance function is a simple model that expresses the variance as a function of the expected value of the survey estimate. The parameters of the generalized variance function are estimated using direct replicate variances. These generalized variance parameters provide a relatively easy method to obtain approximate standard errors for numerous characteristics. Table D-2 provide the generalized variance parameters for FHWAR data. Methods for using the parameters to calculate standard errors of various estimates are given in the next sections.

Standard Errors of Estimated Numbers. The approximate standard error, s_x, of an estimat d number shown in this report can be obtained using the following formulas Formula (1) is used to calculate the standard errors of levels of sportspersons, anglers, and wildlife watchers

$$s_x = \sqrt{ax^2 + bx} \tag{1}$$

Here, x is the size of the estimate and a and b re the parameters in the tables ass ciated with the particular haracteristic

Formula (2) is used for standard error of aggregates, i.e , trips, days, and expenditu es

$$s_x = \sqrt{ax^2 + bx + \frac{cx^2}{y}} \tag{2}$$

Here, x is again the size of the estimate; y is the base of the estimate; and a, b, and c are the parameters in he tables associ ated with the particula characteri ti

Illustration of the Computation of the Standard Error of an Estimated Number

Suppose there were an estimated 37,397,000 persons age 16 years old and older who either fished or hunted in the United States in 20 1 Using formula (1) with the parameters $a = 0.000070$ and $b = 16,823$ from table D 2, the approximate standard error of th estimated number of 37,397,000 sportspersons age 6 y a s old and older is

$$s_x = \sqrt{-0.000070 * 37,397,000^2 + 16,823 * 37,397,000} = 728,857$$

The 95-percent confidence interval for the estimated number of sportspersons 16 years old and older is from 35,968,000 to 38,826,000, i.e., 37,397,000 ± 1.96 x 728,857. Therefore, a conclusion that the average estimate derived from all possible samples lies within a range computed in this way would be correct for roughly 95 percent of all possible samples.

Suppose there were an estimated 13,674,000 hunters age 16 years old and older who engaged in 281,884,000 days of participation in 2011. Using formula (2) with the parameters a = –0.000284, b = –127,863, and c = 46,699 from table D 2, the approximate standard error on 281,884,000 estimated days on an estimated base of 13,674,000 hunters is

$$s_x = \sqrt{-0.000284 * 281,884,000^2 - 127,863 * 281,884,000 + \frac{46,699 * 281,884,000^2}{13,674,000}} = 14,586,000$$

The 95-percent confidence interval on the estimate of 281,884,000 days is from 253,295,000 to 310,473,000, i.e., 281,884,000 ± 1.96 x 14,586,000. Again, a conclusion that the average estimate derived from all possible samples lies within a range computed in this way would be correct for roughly 95 percent of all possible samples.

Standard Errors of Estimated Percentages. The reliability of an estimated percentage, computed using sample data for both numerator and denominator, depends on the size of the percentage and its base. Estimated percentages are relatively more reliable than the corresponding estimates of the numerators of the percentages, particularly if the percentages are 50 percent or more. When the numerator and the denominator of the percentage are in different categories, use the parameter in the tables indicated by the numerator.

The approximate standard error, $s_{x,p}$, can be obtained by use of the formula

$$s_{x,p} = \sqrt{\frac{bp(100 - p)}{x}} \tag{3}$$

Here, x is the total number of sportspersons, hunters, etc., which is the base of the percentage; p is the percentage; and b is the parameter in the tables associated with the characteristic in the numerator of the percentage.

Illustration of the Computation of the Standard Error of an Estimated Percentage

Suppose there were an estimated 13,674,000 hunters age 16 years old and older of whom 18.9 percent hunted migratory birds. From table D-2, the appropriate b parameter is 15,798. Using formula (3), the approximate standard error on the estimate of 18.9 percent is

$$s_{x,p} = \sqrt{\frac{15,798 * 18.9 * (100 - 18.9)}{13,674,000}} = 1.33$$

Consequently, the 95 perc nt confidence interval for the es imate per entage f migrato y bird hunters 16 years old and older is from 16.3 percent to 21.5 percent, i e 18 9 ± 1 96 x 1 33

Standard Error of a Difference The standard error of the differen e b tween two sample estimates is approximately equal to

$$s_{x-y} = \sqrt{s_x^2 + s_y^2} \tag{4}$$

where s_x and s_y are the standard errors f the stimat s x and y The estimates can be numbers, percentages ratios etc. This will represent the actual standard e ror quite ccurately for the di ference between estimat s of the s me characteristi in two different area or for the difference between separate and uncorre ated characteristics in the same ar a However if there is a high positive (negative) corr lation between the two characteristi s, he formula will overestimate (underestimate) the true standard error

Illustration of the Computation of the Standard Error of a Difference

Suppose there w re an estimated 13 608,000 fema es in the age range of 18-24 of whom 726,000 or 5 3 per ent were sportspersons Similarly, suppos there were an estimated 12 909,000 males in the same age range of whom 2,160,000 or 16.7 percent we e sportspersons The apparent difference between the pe centage of female and m le sportspersons is 11 4 percent. Using formula (3) and the appropriate *b* parameter from table D 2 the approximate standard errors of 5 3 per ent and 16.7 pe cent are 0 79 and 1 35, re pectively Us ng formula (4), the approximate standard error of the estimated difference of 11.4 percent is

$$s_{x-y} = \sqrt{0.79^2 + 1.35^2} = 1.56$$

The 95-percent confidence interval on he difference between 18 to 24 year-old female and male sportspersons is from 8 3 to 14.5, i e 11 4 ± 1 96 x 1 56 Since the interval does not contain zero we can conclude with 95 percent confidence that the percentage f 18 to 24 year-old female sportsper ons is less than the percentage of 18 to 24-year old male sportspersons.

Standard Errors of Estimated Averages Certain mean value for sportspersons, anglers et shown in the report were calcu lated as the r tio of two numbers. For example, ave age days per angler is calculated as

$$\frac{x}{y} = \frac{total\ days}{total\ anglers}$$

Standard errors for these averages may be approximated by the use of formula (5) below.

$$s_{x/y} = \frac{x}{y} \sqrt{\left[\frac{s_x}{x}\right]^2 + \left[\frac{s_y}{y}\right]^2 - 2r\frac{s_x s_y}{xy}} \tag{5}$$

In formula (5), *r* represents the correlation coefficient between the numerator and the denominator of the estimate In the above formula, use 0.7 as an estimate of *r*.

Illustration of the Computation of the Standard Error of an Estimated Average

Suppose that the estimated number of the average days per angler age 16 years old and older for all fishing was 16.7 days Using formulas (1) and (2) above, we compute the standard error on total days, 553,841,000, and total anglers, 33,112,000, to be 20,329,124 and 693 033, respectively The approximate standard error on the estimated average of 16.7 days is

$$s_{x/y} = \frac{553,841,000}{33,112,000} \sqrt{\left[\frac{20,329,124}{553,841,000}\right]^2 + \left[\frac{693,033}{33,112,000}\right]^2 - 2 * 0.7 \frac{20,329,124 * 693,033}{553,841,000 * 33,112,000}} = 0.45$$

Therefore, the 95-percent confidence interval on the estimated average of 16.7 days is from 15.8 to 17 6, i.e., 16.7 ± 1.96 x 0 45.

Table D-1. Approximate Standard Errors for Indiana State Resident Anglers, Hunters, and Away-from-Home Wildlife Watchers

(Numbers in thousands)

Resident anglers, hunters, and away-from-home wildlife watchers	Estimate	Standard error
Resident Anglers		
Participation	786	82
Spenders[1]	757	81
Days of fishing	21,502	6,437
Expenditures in dollars	649,164	199,166
Resident Hunters		
Participation	377	63
Spenders[1]	368	62
Days of hunting	10,902	3,530
Expenditures in dollars	209,736	75,017
Resident Away-from-Home Wildlife Watchers		
Participation	477	66
Spenders[1]	408	61
Days away-from-home wildlife watching	3,552	827
Trip-related expenditures in dollars	404,132	192,082

[1] The spenders estimate for resident anglers and resident hunters is all participants who bought equipment and trip-related items. The spenders estimate for away-from-home wildlife watchers is all participants who bought trip-related items

Table D-2. Parameters a, b, and c for Calculating Approximate Standard Errors for U.S. and Indiana Screener, Detailed Sportsperson, and Wildlife-Watching Samples for Levels, Expenditures, and Days or Trips

Sample	Parameters					
	United States			Indiana		
	a	b	c	a	b	c
Screener Sample						
Sportspersons, anglers, hunters, and wildlife-watching participants 6 years old and older	−0 000043	12,272	(X)	−0 000849	4,951	(X)
Sportspersons, anglers, hunters, and wildlife-watching participants 6 to 15 years old	−0 000387	15,783	(X)	−0 012557	10,925	(X)
Detailed Sportsperson Sample						
Sportspersons and anglers 16 years old and older	−0 000070	16,823	(X)	−0 002038	10,118	(X)
Hunters 16 years old and older	−0 000066	15,798	(X)	−0 002294	11,391	(X)
Expenditures for sportspersons and anglers 16 years old and older	0 001159	−575,615	45,670	0 084408	56,304	7,293
Expenditures for hunters 16 years old and older	0 001923	−978,460	44,416	0 113115	42,035	5,378
Days or trips for sportspersons and anglers 16 years old and older	0 000068	−160,414	51,951	0 079426	−2,044	8,077
Days or trips for hunters 16 years old and older	−0 000284	−127,863	46,699	0 088709	7,770	5,819
Wildlife-Watching Sample						
Levels of wildlife-watching—away-from-home participants	−0 000134	32,078	(X)	−0 002020	10,030	(X)
Levels of wildlife-watching—wildlife-watching participants[1]	−0 000119	28,477	(X)	−0 006775	33,637	(X)
Expenditures for wildlife-watching	0 001308	−1,548,024	112,362	0 193872	−322,885	13,396
Days or trips for wildlife-watching	0 002307	826,023	54,100	−0 040883	−166,121	69,136

(X) Not applicable

[1] Use these parameters for total wildlife-watching participants and around-the-home participants

U.S. Department of the Interior
U.S. Fish & Wildlife Service

http://wsfrprograms.fws.gov

March 2013